TEACHING YOUR CHILD

· · · · · · · · · · to · · · · · · · · · ·

READ

A Parent's Guide to Encouraging a Love of Reading

JESSICA WANG & LU JUN

Skyhorse Publishing

First Skyhorse Publishing edition, 2022
Published in agreement with Jilin Publishing Group Co., Ltd.

Skyhorse Publishing books may be purchased in bulk at special discounts for sales promotion, corporate gifts, fund-raising, or educational purposes. Special editions can also be created to specifications. For details, contact the Special Sales Department, Skyhorse Publishing, 307 West 36th Street, 11th Floor, New York, NY 10018 or info@skyhorsepublishing.com.

Skyhorse® and Skyhorse Publishing® are registered trademarks of Skyhorse Publishing, Inc.®, a Delaware corporation.

Visit our website at www.skyhorsepublishing.com.

10 9 8 7 6 5 4 3 2 1

Library of Congress Cataloging-in-Publication Data is available on file.

Cover design by Daniel Brount
Cover images: Shutterstock
English edition editorial consultant: Weihua Liu

Print ISBN: 978-1-5107-6433-0
Ebook ISBN: 978-1-5107-6434-7

Printed in the United States of America

Contents

Preface: Reading Is a Skill to Be Learned   **vii**

**Chapter 1: How to Get Kids Interested in Reading
in the First Place**   **1**

Intermittent questioning approach: Why aren't kids
engaged when you read picture books with them?   1

Picture-to-object approach: How do children go
from reading pictures to advanced reading?   7

Page-to-detail approach: How can you guide the child's
attention to picture details?   15

Emotion comparison card: How to let the kids feel the
emotions of book characters   23

**Chapter 2: How to Improve Kids' Reading Participation
Through Basic Training**   **32**

Content repetition approach: How do we use
recurring things in a book?   32

Imagination and attention management:
How to let children better use their imagination   39

Immersive-reading approach: What should we do
    when kids can't concentrate on reading?   47
Speculation approach: How to make kids more
    engaged in reading   54

**Chapter 3: How to Improve Kids' Reading
Concentration and Consistency**   **60**
Plot-connection approach: Why kids forget what
    they just read   60
Ritual-of-reading approach: How to inspire respect
    for reading   67
Stepped-lead-in reading: Does word-by-word
    reading really help?   74
Phased-targeting approach: How to make reading
    as addictive as playing games   80

Chapter 4: How to Develop Good Reading Habits   **86**
Word-locking approach: Can preschool children
    learn to recognize words?   86
Family story party: How to motivate kids to read more   93
Alternate reading: How to nail knowledge in children's
    minds   101
Reciting fluently: What are the benefits of reading aloud?   108

Chapter 5: Training Children's Basic Reading Ability   **116**
Role play: What is children's true understanding of books?   116
Q&A games: How to cultivate children's ability
    to think independently   123
Expert guidance: What roles should parents play
    in parent-child reading?   131

Behavior adjustment: How to apply book learning
   in real life   136

Chapter 6: Training Children's Comprehensive
  Reading Ability   **144**
  Milestone method: When to pick harder books
    for children   144
  Collation of clues: What to do if children fear to
    read books with complex plots   151
  Plot map: How to teach children to read heavy books   157
  Imagination and verification: How to mobilize
    children's initiative for reading   166

Chapter 7: Training Children's Expressive Ability
  Based on Reading   **172**
  Rehearsal exercise: Why children can't retell after
    reading so many books   172
  Jump-back rehearsal: What to do if children often
    forget when retelling stories   179
  Adaptation and continuation: Should we encourage
    children to invent stories when reading?   185
  Comprehensive output: Why children can't write
    good essays even after reading many books   193

Further Reading   **200**
Index   **202**

Preface

Reading Is a Skill to Be Learned

When it comes to reading, what would be the first thing that comes to mind? Back in the day, I thought that reading was all about word recognition, and one naturally reads better by learning more words. Not until I started to learn early childhood education curriculum did I realize that I was completely wrong. Reading is in fact a skill, or even a competence to be developed by learning throughout one's lifetime.

I live in New York, where children start to receive graded reading materials in elementary school. Teachers lead the children to read and teach them how to use reading tools. Moreover, during the summer and winter vacations, there are reading activities arranged by schools and public libraries, showing how much the people here value reading.

By communicating with some parents, I've learned that, for them, cultivation of reading ability is still a somewhat elusive concept. A few of these parents understand that the development of reading ability is a systematic process based on certain rules, but are struggling to find graded reading materials proven to be good. As a result, these parents scrape together whatever books they can find, without knowing if they are actually suitable for their kids' development at the current stage. Other parents know reading is good for kids, so they just keep buying more books. However, in the end, they find that their kids still have no interest in reading and all the picture books they bought are just collecting dust in the corners. At this point, the parents are starting to wonder: What's going on? Why doesn't my kid like reading?

So what exactly is reading ability? As a matter of fact, it can't be simply put as the ability to read or finish a book, and its development is a systematic process based on scientific rules, which involve the learning of a set of reading tools that correspond to specific stages of brain and cognitive development. For most people, the development of reading ability can be divided into three stages. The first stage is "learning how to read," which goes from one's birth to the third grade; the second stage, called "learning by reading," lasts from the third grade to the twelfth grade; while the third one, called "act by reading," starts from entering into college to coming of age.

Ever since my daughter D was born, I have been paying particular attention to her reading. Our parent-child reading has been going on for five years so far, and I have been studying early childhood education in New York for almost three years. At the same time, I've also been learning about brain science and neuroscience from experts in New York. Over the years, I have found that helping a child learn reading is really not a simple matter, because it is closely related to psychology, pedagogy, brain science, and cognitive science. Almost all children can learn to speak without much effort, but none can learn to read in the same manner. To complete a reading task, we need to simultaneously use the brain's language circuit and another section of the brain responsible for image recognition. More often than not, lack of reading tools and environmental support designed according to scientific principles make a child fail at reading. The tools and abilities required for reading are like "pearls" scattered all over the place, and stringing them into a beautiful "necklace" requires parents to collect each one of them through learning, perception, and even some comprehensive study. Only by such efforts can we as parents be ready to pass on the knowledge to our children in a step-by-step manner. It's easy to see why reading education is a daunting task for most parents.

Based on the above understanding, I began to wonder if it would be possible to summarize a set of practical reading methods based on my experience of five years of parent-child reading and what I had learned from my more than three years of study. I wanted to share it with more parents who value parent child reading to make it easier for them to overcome the obstacles in reading education.

With this idea in mind, and through my work with Cuckoo Learning as well as more than thirty top parent-child reading experts in China, I've created twenty-eight reading methods designed for children from three to six years old. These lessons are derived from a program I helped create in China called "Graded Reading on Good Character and Scholarship for Chinese Children," but I believe they are applicable for learning to read the English language, as well.

Reading is a skill that needs to be learned. The inheritance of such a skill requires us, as parents, to take action.

—Jessica Wang
New York

Chapter 1
How to Get Kids Interested in Reading in the First Place

Intermittent questioning approach: Why aren't kids engaged when you read picture books with them?

First of all, we must break down a misunderstanding that kids love it when you tell stories to them. In fact, there is no direct connection between storytelling and a kid's enjoyment. Kids listening to stories is not much different than an adult listening to a colleague talking about work stuff; it's just a method of passive information reception. When a child hears a "story," their brain first begins to decode the text and extract the semantics, and then they try to understand the things they heard by putting them into context. Such a process will ultimately lead to the engagement of emotion-related brain sections such as the amygdala and hippocampus. It's after going through all those brain activities that the child will finally arrive at a conclusion, which would be either "it's quite interesting" or "I'm not interested."

The key to deciding whether a child is interested in the story lies in the process of their brain activity. If you are just focused on finishing the story, leaving no time for a kid's brain to decode the text and extract semantic meaning, it's only natural for them to stop trying to understand and do something else instead. If such a pattern continues, it could, in the worst case, cause a child to lose interest in reading. To put things into your own perspective, if you fail to do and finish something over and over again, over time you won't feel like giving it another go. In psychology, this situation is often referred to as "learned helplessness."

As such, what we should do is control the rhythm of reading so that the kid has time to think. For example, we can pause and wait a while when there is something that is hard to understand or needs some time to sink in. To do this, we can call for help in an approach called "Intermittent Questioning."

🌟

What is "Intermittent Questioning"? Obviously, "Questioning" means you asking your kid questions. What about the term "Intermittent"? It means the alternation between two questioning methods, "mid-way questioning" and "holistic questioning." The former refers to making appropriate pauses in the middle of repeated storytelling so that questions about a certain detail can be raised; while the latter refers to asking kids questions about the key content of the story upon the completion of story reading. In the following text, we use two picture book stories as examples to illustrate the specific application of this approach.

Taking *Molly Goes Shopping* as an example, how do we use "mid-way questioning" with this book? When telling the story about Molly buying the wrong thing on her first trip, after reaching the point where Molly's grandma has learned Molly's mistake and returned home, you should take a pause and ask your kid, "Where does Molly hide?" "Why do you think she is in hiding?" By such step-by-step questioning, we can guide the kids to talk about their understanding of the plot and to realize by themselves that lying is shameful. Then, upon telling the story about Molly's second errand, you can ask your kid, "What should Molly buy this time? What has she actually bought?" which can be followed by questions such as: "Why did Grandma say Molly bought the right things?" "Do you agree with her?" By asking such questions, we can test the kids' awareness and perception of certain details of the story. Also, since these questions are quite easy to answer, the kids can easily get to the right answers and enjoy the sense of success.

What about holistic questioning? Still using *Molly Goes Shopping* as an example, after finishing the entire story with the child, you can ask them: "Do you remember how many times Molly bought something?" "When did Molly buy the right thing, and when did she make a mistake?" "Molly bought things and went home twice. Why did Grandma rush out for the first time, but praise Molly the second time?" It can be seen that holistic questioning covers more information. Answering such questions is more difficult for children, because it requires the comprehensive use of a variety of abilities such as understanding, judgment, and induction. We can use "intermediate questioning" and "holistic questioning" alternately to let the children practice with different abilities.

It should be noted that when asking questions you should use a gentle tone and not make it a test. If the child can't answer, don't lose patience, just go through the corresponding page again with them or help them recall the story line. You should never say something like, "How can you forget? You are so stupid!" The purpose of the questioning methods described in this section is not making children learn knowledge and memorize things, but to let them learn and love reading.

If we don't have the book *Molly Goes Shopping*, how can we use the questioning methods on other books? To do this, we need to apply questioning techniques. Here are four universal tips for using the questioning methods:

Tip 1: Try to use open-ended questions and avoid using general questions. If parents always ask their children when telling a story: "Is it right?" "Is it OK?" or "Is it good or bad?" then the children can only answer "yes" or "no," and there is no way for them to really think deeply. If we adopt open-ended questions such as "If you were him, what would you do?" "If your mother was like her, what would you think?" the effects will be far better. Taking *Molly Goes Shopping* as an example, we can use open-ended questions such as: "If you were Molly and bought the wrong thing, what would you do?"

Tip 2: There should be a connection between the questions. Taking the picture book *Giggle King's Big Hat* as an example, when reading or hearing about the first appearance of Giggle King, in which he is sitting on a round cake tree, we can ask the child: "What do you think Giggle King is feeling right now?" and when reaching the end of the story line, ask them, "How is Giggle King feeling now that he has made a bunch of friends?" If your child tells you that Giggle King's mood has changed, you can ask them: "Why do you think that?" You can see that all three questions are connected, and this kind of contextual questioning helps to deepen children's understanding of the story and to effectively train their thinking ability.

Tip 3: Maintain an appropriate questioning frequency. We know that asking questions helps, but it does not mean we should keep asking questions during the storytelling process, as that would ruin the reading experience completely. The key to questioning is in quality, not quantity, so we just need to raise questions when the story reaches a critical or important point. At the beginning of using the intermittent questioning approach, you should just ask one question for each story and then gradually increase the number of questions for each story over time. Parents also need to observe their children's response when asking questions. If the child has no response after hearing a question, it's may be because the question is not good or the child is too tired to think. At this time, parents should try another way of questioning, and if such adjustment does not work, they can temporarily stop using the questioning method and wait until the next parent-child reading session.

Tip 4: Ask questions based on the theme of the picture book. Each picture book has a corresponding theme, and these themes often involve problems that children will encounter as they grow up, or their perception of the world. The purpose of reading picture books is to continuously expand children's knowledge of themselves and everything in the world and gain insights that can affect their personal growth. Therefore, after getting a picture book, parents should think of questions based on what the author wants to convey through the book's story. Take *Giggle King's Big Hat* as an example. After reading the story, you can ask your child: "Now do you understand what loneliness means?" Of course, parents can also add their own thoughts on the theme of the book when asking questions to enrich their children's understanding, and such questioning can be seen as a form of in-depth parent-child communication.

Summary

"Intermittent questioning" means the use of two questioning methods, "mid-way questioning" and "holistic questioning." The former refers to making appropriate pauses in the middle of storytelling so that questions about a certain detail can be raised, and the latter refers to asking kids questions about the key content of the story upon the completion of story reading. When using intermittent questioning, it's recommended for parents to use open-ended questions and those having contextual connections, maintain an appropriate questioning frequency, and focus on the theme of the picture book. The next time you read a book with your child, please make sure to think of some questions based on the story and use the intermittent questioning approach in the reading process to inspire your kid to think and learn.

Picture-to-object approach: How do children go from reading pictures to advanced reading?

Picture-to-Object Approach

Taking the picture-to-object approach means that we use picture books as reference materials and look for real-life objects depicted in them, so that the kids can associate things in the artworks with corresponding real-world objects. In this way, we can help the children learn how to effectively compare pictures and objects, understand image symbols, and perform abstract thinking.

As the name implies, the picture-to-object approach means that we use picture books as reference materials and look for real-life objects depicted in them, so that the kids associate things expressed through various art techniques with corresponding real-world objects. In this way, we can help the children learn how to effectively compare pictures and objects. Why do we need to pay particular attention to this approach? It's because the ability to associate pictures with real-life objects is required for improving a kid's picture reading, and the ability to read pictures is a most basic reading skill. Why do we say that? What are the principles of brain science behind this assertion?

We know that pictures depict the real world with different levels of abstraction. Let's take apples as an example. Below are nine pictures of apples, in which the degree of abstraction gradually increases (from photograph to drawings and symbols). Let's take a closer look.

The first picture is a photo of a real apple (Figure 1). Compared to three-dimensional (3D), augmented-reality (AR), and virtual-reality (VR) versions of apples, a photo is just a flat two-dimensional depiction of the real thing. In fact, in terms of information related to the apple, a photo embodies a certain degree of abstraction, because it only shows the front of the apple, and we can't see the side and back of it or glean additional information about its smell and taste. In can be said that photograph is also a form of abstract expression, but the level of abstraction is very low.

The second picture is a realistic oil painting (Figure 2). Compared to photos, a painting can't show a lot of information about the apple and its leaf, including color, light, shadow, and texture. However, for the kids, it still looks very much like an apple. So, as a form of abstract expression, an oil painting takes a step further than photograph, but only a minor step.

Figure 1   Figure 2

The third picture is a vector illustration of an apple with light and shadow effects (Figure 3). Compared to the textured oil painting, this picture loses most information about the apple other than its shape and color and a little bit of light and shadow on it. However, it is still relatively easy for children to recognize that this is an apple.

The fourth picture is an anthropomorphic cartoon image of an apple (Figure 4). Compared to the third picture, this cartoon image retains only the shape and color of the apple without showing any light and shadow, but with the addition of a face with expression. As such, it can be said that this image is an adapted reproduction of the real thing. However, some people have found through experiments that compared with vector graphics, children are more likely to recognize what such cartoon images represent. This may be because that children tend to be good at recognizing faces.

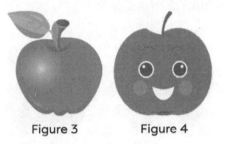

Figure 3   Figure 4

The fifth (Figure 5) and seventh (Figure 7) pictures are line drawings of an apple. As a very abstract form of expression, stick figures use contours and lines to show the real thing, with or without colors. Obviously, colored stick figures are more recognizable to children.

The sixth (Figure 6) picture is an abstract illustration of an apple's color and shape, depicting the contour of a green apple with strokes of green color. It has no lines, only the shape and color. As another form of abstract expression, this picture is more difficult for children to recognize.

Figure 5   Figure 6   Figure 7

The eighth (Figure 8) and ninth (Figure 9) images are brand logos of Apple. Both of them are symbolized illustrations of the real thing, one in 3D with color and textures, and the other in black and white vector-graph. For a child who has never seen the logo of an Apple product, it requires some abstract thinking and imagination to recognize that either of these two pictures is an apple that has a bite taken out of it.

Figure 8   Figure 9

All nine pictures are abstract illustrations of a real apple. However, the ones with higher degrees of abstraction are more difficult to recognize. No child is born with the ability to recognize processed images of various forms. For children, it takes the learning of abstract thinking to recognize abstract illustrations that are entirely plain and simple for adults. The picture-to-object approach introduced here is a reading tool that can help children learn to establish a connection between the real world and the abstract works.

From the perspective of the science behind reading skills, reading-comprehension ability can be divided into two parts: The first is picture reading and comprehension, which are required to do picture talks. The second is text reading and comprehension, which are required for reading text books. Taking the picture-to-object approach marks the first step in a child's learning of picture reading and comprehension. People who lack adequate training in picture reading beginning in childhood may have difficulty understanding graphics when they reach adulthood. For example, there are some adults who find it hard to understand warning signs in public places and those who often misread traffic signs when driving. We can see that, unlike the prevailing notion that pictures are just there to illustrate the meaning of words, picture books actually serve an important purpose of allowing the children to practice "picture reading."

❧

As stated in the book *Supercharge a Kid's Brainpower*, it takes eight steps for child to fall in love with reading.

Table 1: Eight Steps of Learning to Read

Step 1	Know what a book is
Step 2	Take the first step
Step 3	Start noticing the pictures
Step 4	Notice what the reader says are related to the pictures
Step 5	Learn to understand the story
Step 6	Learn to retell the story
Step 7	Get interested in text
Step 8	Start reading independently

By going through eight such steps, children can gradually obtain the five most essential skills for reading. The first of these is to establish connections, which corresponds to the picture-to-object approach.

In the text below, the book *Peter's Chair* is taken as an example to show you how the picture-to-object approach can be applied in real life to help children develop imaginative thinking and abstract thinking skills.

Step 1: Find the keyword, which is the name of the real thing. The keyword for *Peter's Chair* is "chair." Since the cover of the book has a blue chair in it, after picking up the book, you can tell your child that the book tells the story of a chair and start using the picture-to-object tool. Ask the child: "Do we have a chair at home?" If the child immediately replies, "Of course we do," it means they have begun to associate the chair in the picture with chairs in real life.

Step 2: Ask your child questions. You can ask them, "How many chairs do we have at home?" then see what kinds of chairs your child can think of (such as dining chairs, children's chairs, office chairs, folding chairs, rocking chairs, etc.). Next, you can continue to ask your child: "Which chairs have you seen elsewhere?" and measure your kid's abstract and inductive thinking ability based on the answers given. After the child tells you about various chairs, you can then ask them to do a simple classification of chairs according to different dimensions (shape, height, color, texture, etc.). Through the above process, most children will remember one thing that these things we use to sit have different appearances and functional characteristics, they are all called "chairs," which means that they now understand the word "chair" as an abstract concept.

Step 3: Guide your child to make comparisons. When reading *Peter's Chair* with your child, in addition to letting them pay attention to the story line, you should also guide them to observe the height, color, and shape of the chairs in the story and compare them with real chairs at home to find similarities and differences between them. Two chairs appeared in the book, a high chair (a dining chair that Peter once used) and a small one. Both were blue at first, but dad wants to paint them pink after Peter's sister was born so that she can use them. At this point, Peter gets angry at his dad for giving something of his to his sister and runs away from home. In the end of the story, Peter finds that the small chair was too small for him, and it's something that he can't use but his sister needs the most. At this moment, Peter realizes his mistake and decides to paint the small chair pink with his father so they can give it to his sister. After reading the entire story, you can inspire your child to think by asking, "Why was Peter angry at first but then willing to give the chair to his sister?" In this way, the child not only gets to practice image thinking and abstract thinking but also learns about empathy and sharing with others.

The picture-to-object approach has many extended uses, including helping children learn words. Still taking apples as an example, the picture-to-object approach can also be used in various forms to teach children the word "apple," including recalling various apples that we have eaten and seen in life; going online to search for photos of various apples and looking at them with the children; looking for artworks that involve apples; and finally, guiding the child to really understand how to associate things in real life with their counterparts in various forms of representation including text narrative. Many flash cards that have words on one side and pictures on the other are good examples for comparing physical objects and their abstract counterparts. Parents can even make similar flash cards with their children based on the picture-to-object approach.

In addition to *Peter's Chair*, many other picture books in our graded reading list, such as *My Dad!*, *The Gruffalo*, and *Martine on the Farm*, are also very suitable for application of the picture-to-object approach. The dad in *My Dad!*, the buffalo in *The Gruffalo*, and various small animals in *Martine on the Farm* are all good examples of abstract objects with easy-to-find real-life counterparts.

I hope that parents can think of more ways to effectively train their children's abstract thinking and image thinking skills with the help of the picture-to-object approach and picture books already at hand, so as to improve the kids' reading comprehension step-by-step and help them fall in love with reading faster and gradually gain the ability to read autonomously.

Summary

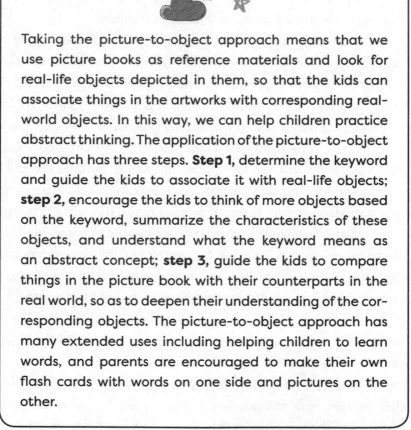

Taking the picture-to-object approach means that we use picture books as reference materials and look for real-life objects depicted in them, so that the kids can associate things in the artworks with corresponding real-world objects. In this way, we can help children practice abstract thinking. The application of the picture-to-object approach has three steps. **Step 1,** determine the keyword and guide the kids to associate it with real-life objects; **step 2,** encourage the kids to think of more objects based on the keyword, summarize the characteristics of these objects, and understand what the keyword means as an abstract concept; **step 3,** guide the kids to compare things in the picture book with their counterparts in the real world, so as to deepen their understanding of the corresponding objects. The picture-to-object approach has many extended uses including helping children to learn words, and parents are encouraged to make their own flash cards with words on one side and pictures on the other.

Page-to-detail approach: How can you guide the child's attention to picture details?

Page-to-Detail Approach

Taking the page-to-detail approach means that parents first point to an entire page of the picture book and give their children a clear overview of things happening on that page, then guide their children to focus on specific picture details on the same page, and talk with the children about what they see in the picture.

How do we decide if a book for kindergarten kids is good or not? To answer this question, Mr. Xiong Liang, a famous picture book master, suggested that although we can use many indicators to measure the quality of children's books, the most important and essential indicator should always be: How much dialogue space does a book provide to the parents and their children with its pictures and stories? Mr. Xiong Liang believes that a good picture book should provide more opportunities for dialogue between parents and children. If a child has no chance to ask questions and talk about them by the time a picture book is finished, we can say this book is no good at all. Parent-child reading is not just about adults reading the book and telling kids what's happening while the children listen passively. Anyone who believes that would be wasting a golden opportunity to inspire the kids to observe and learn.

Now we know picture books should allow for more parent-children interaction, but how can we make practical use of such interactivity during daily parent-child reading? In fact, in scientific research on reading and cognition, interactivity is often brought up, along with an important reading tool referred to as the "page-to-detail approach."

Why does using this page-to-detail tool help parents and children interact more during book reading? It's because the basic logic behind it is that by means of comparison and observation, the kids can find interesting clues about relevance, difference, and causal relationship between things observed from the whole page and specific details in it.

For example, when kids see cats and tigers in picture books, they may start to wonder why these two animals look alike, and if they realize that it's because a cat and a tiger are both felines, they have found a correlation. For another example, when seeing dolphins and sharks in picture books, kids may find a difference when they realize that although dolphins and sharks all live in the ocean, they actually belong to two different groups of animals (mammals and fishes). For yet another example, when seeing waterfalls in picture books, kids may find a causal relationship between height difference (between water surfaces) and waterfall when they realize that the latter is caused by the former.

During parent-child reading, we need to select picture books that allow kids to ask more questions and find more page-to-detail links. Only by using those books can we effectively inspire children to observe, compare, imagine, analyze, evaluate, and form opinions, which is consistent with the cognitive science principles behind the reading tool collection. But just knowing the principles does not help us solve the problem of improving children's reading ability; we also need to know how to apply them.

Simply put, taking the page-to-detail approach means that parents first point to an entire page of the picture book and give their children a clear overview of things happening on that page, then guide their children to focus on specific picture details on the same page and talk with them about what they see in the picture. Note that this approach doesn't involve "point to read," because in order to guide the kids to observe the images, the parents should point to the pictures on the page instead of the text. Other than promoting the development of basic skills, taking the page-to-detail approach also helps the children get a sense of the overall structure of the content of the picture book. In other words, we can guide the children to understand through their own observation how book contents are organized, much like picturing a building's architectural plans or those of a load-bearing structure by looking at it from the outside and distinguishing between different building parts such as frame construction and soft and hard decoration.

Moreover, taking the page-to-detail approach can also help children clearly understand the main plots and core themes of a book, the author's main point of view, and presentation of details as well as to identify primary and secondary keywords of the book. The ability to extract such information is key to improving children's reading skills. In the text below, several stories taken from picture books included in "Graded Reading on Good Character and Scholarship" are used as reference materials to introduce specific ways to apply the page-to-detail approach in practice and how to use this tool to improve children's reading ability.

First, Barbara Cooney's masterpiece *Miss Rumphius* is taken as an example to introduce specific steps of using the page-to-detail approach.

Step 1: Guide the child to take a look at the whole picture by hovering your finger over the page, and then ask the kid "What's this page about?" The cover page of *Miss Rumphius* is a very good example for interactive questioning during parent-child reading. First, let the child take an overall look of the cover page, seeing that it presents a small hill by the sea, which is covered by green meadow. The child may first notice a detail on the hill: There is a woman standing upwind on the hill, and her cloak is slightly lifted by the gentle breeze, revealing a purple skirt underneath. And the woman appears to be walking with her head held high. Well, if the child replies to your first question by saying: "There is a woman here," it means that they have noticed this detail. We can then try to draw the child's attention from the detail back to the overall picture by asking: "Where does she stand?" This question will turn the kid's eyes back to the hill, but this time with the woman on it. Then we continue to raise questions such as "Who is she? Is she Miss Rumphius? Where is she going? Is she facing the sea? Is she going home or just for a walk by the sea?" The child may want to answer these questions and is now filled with guesses, meaning that they are ready to read the entire picture book with you. However, at this stage, some kids may have other ideas than just hearing out the story, so we need to be patient. You can pick up the book and spread open its front and back covers so that the two pages are combined into a larger picture, then point to this combined picture and let the child see that the woman is walking toward the sea. Next, you continue by swiping your finger along the winding footpath under the woman's feet, guiding the child's sight and attention toward another small hill in the upper left corner of the picture and a house on it. By now, the child should have taken a look at the entire picture and found the answers to all the questions just raised. For children, such a process of finding the answers is quite rewarding, and they will want to continue reading because they like the feel of taking an active part in exploring the story.

Step 2: Focus on the picture details and guide the child to find the connections between different details. Ask your child what correlations, similarities, and causality they can find by exploring all the clues in the pictures' details. For example, you can guide the child to observe details of the house in the picture by asking them: "What did you see? Does the house by the sea have a balcony?" If the kid says "yes," you then ask, "Does the house have a yard?" The child will say that the house has a yard made of stones, and its entrance is a gray fence. Next, you continue by asking, "Are there any plants other than grass in this picture?" The child will soon notice that there are four big trees around the house, upon which point you can say: "What about other places in the picture?" which will prompt them to find other trees located on the far side of the island. By such a process of progressive inquiry, we've guided the child to notice a lot of details in the picture, including plants such as grasses and trees, and let them find clues to the answers to questions such as, "Is the woman walking toward the sea?" (by looking at which way she is facing), and "Is she going home or just for a walk?" (by measuring the distance between the woman and the house). We can see that, by guiding the child through the above process, we've managed to help them practice the abilities to observe, compare, imagine, analyze, evaluate, and measure.

Step 3: Repeat the first two steps. After turning to the title page of the book (the one with lupines), first you still guide the child to see the picture as a whole, telling them what lupines look like or showing them photos of lupines on the internet, and letting them know that the lupine is a native North American plant generally growing in sandy land with moderate temperatures. From here, you can repeat the process in the first two steps, using your fingers to guide the child to find correlations between each picture as a whole and its details as well as to inspire them to observe carefully.

Step 4: Relational comparison. This is the last step after finishing the book: Guide the child to do a relational comparison between the theme of the book and specific details on various pages. The purpose of such comparison is to inspire the child to learn to correlate information obtained from different pages and to recognize and understand things from more than one perspective. Still taking *Miss Rumphius* as an example, you can ask the child: "How many times have lupines appeared in the book?" The child will find that in addition to the title page, lupines also appear on the first (in the vase) and the second page (around the house) of the book; and they can be seen in many scenarios throughout the book's story, including lupines outside the window when the lady was in bed due to injury, those on the road when the lady went out for a walk in early spring, and those flourishing around the town's fence. They will see that lupines are everywhere throughout the book. After obtaining the above information, you can tell the child about the author's creation background; that is, where the author lives, there is a legend that a lady called Ms. Lupines who brings seeds of lupines to the world, and beautiful lupines grow everywhere she passes. By seeing that the author created this picture book based on a beautiful legend, the child will understand that the theme of this picture book is to make the world a better place.

We will find out at this time that for young kids, reading picture books can also be a process of self-discovery and exploration. Other than truly feeling the author's love for beautiful things in the world, going through above steps with *Miss Rumphius* can also help the child practice autonomous reading, and such a comprehensive effect would never be achieved by simple instruction.

For three- to six-year-old children, the page-to-detail approach can become a very useful and effective picture book reading aid. I hope you can use it to truly achieve high-quality parent-child reading.

Summary

To apply the page-to-detail tool, parents need to use their fingers to guide the children to observe each picture as a whole and its various details (excluding text). In addition to exercising various basic abilities (such as observation and imagination), using the page-to-detail tool can also help children understand the overall structure of a picture book's content and improve their ability to compare, analyze, and measure complex things. The application of the page-to-detail approach contains four steps: **Step 1,** guide the child to observe each picture as a whole; **Step 2,** guide the child to observe details in each picture and find out the connections between such details; **Step 3,** finish the entire picture book by repeating the first two steps continuously; **Step 4,** inspire the child to compare and correlate the theme of the book and specific details in it, so as to prepare them for autonomous reading.

Emotion comparison card:
How to let the kids feel the emotions of book characters

Emotion Comparison Card

The emotion comparison card is a reading tool that can be prepared in advance of reading a picture book. To make a basic emotion comparison card, you only need to draw the expressions that show basic emotions such as joy, anger, sadness, and fear on a piece of cardboard. You can use this card when reading the picture book to help the child understand emotions and learn how to handle, control, and make good use of them.

The book *Supercharge a Kid's Brainpower* specifically states that teaching children how to manage emotions is one of the most critical tasks in early childhood education. It can be said that one of the key tasks that most normal people do in their lives is control impulsive emotions with rational and calm minds. Most parents or caregivers have "lost it," or have felt out of control, at one time or another. It can even be said that if not for some people's runaway emotions, many huge disasters in human history may not have happened.

Emotional control is indeed very important. However, it is very normal for young children to lose control of their emotions. Based on current studies of brain science, researchers believe that a child's brain can be divided into five sections according to functions: the intelligence section, the motion control section, the emotion control section, the linguistics section, and the creativity section. Among those five sections, the emotion control section matures latest. It is normal for young children to experience runaway emotions, and we as parents must duly recognize that fact. So, how can we effectively control our emotions? The first step should be accepting the emotions. For example, before the kids say "no" to something, their parents can clearly state to them that "If you . . . I will . . ." as a way to express emotions in advance through language. In addition, we also need to be clear about the difference between emotions and behaviors. That is, emotions are naturally generated, but behaviors can be good or bad. In view of such difference, we cannot allow emotions to dictate our behaviors and must find ways to effectively block the path through which such influence occurs.

There are many ways to effectively promote a child's emotional control brain section to mature gradually, enabling them to take good control of their emotions. Book reading is one of these methods. But how should we use this method to help our kids learn to effectively control their emotions and behaviors? To accept emotions, one must first know the independent existence of different emotions, and it's the reason why we should prepare an emotion comparison card in advance and use it as an auxiliary tool when reading picture books.

Step 1: Prepare the emotion comparison card. Find a piece of cardboard half the size of an A4 paper and draw on it facial expressions indicating laughter, joy, comfort, anger, sadness, being naughty, fear, etc. Below (Figure 10) is a basic emotion comparison card.

Figure 10

Step 2: Help children effectively recognize and understand emotions. To do this, you should choose picture books with stories that have more emotional ups and downs to explore with your kid. During reading, you should ask your kid how each character feels in a specific scenario, and ask them to find the corresponding image(s) on the emotion card and then say the character's dialogue in the scenario, with a tone and facial expression befitting the character's mood in that same scenario. As it is possible for children aged from three to six to practice reading and expressing with emotions even if they don't know any words, it would be even better if your kid can say something based on their own thought, independent of the book content. Practicing the above emotional expressions can help children realize that emotions are by-products of interactions between people and the world and between each person and other people. It also helps the kids to understand that each emotion (sadness, joy, frustration, jealousy, anger, hatred) exists individually and independently. Because the relation between emotions and people is not something a kid can understand without effort, it's easy for them to mistake feelings for facts, thinking that feelings and emotions are inborn. Therefore, to accept emotions, we must first understand that emotions are not physical parts of the human body, and to manage emotions we must first learn to effectively identify different emotions.

Step 3: Let the children learn empathy by exploring the emotional conflicts and confrontations experienced by book characters. In many cases, the serious consequences of runaway emotions are the result of the responsible parties' failure to reasonably assess the impact of their emotions and behaviors on the communities they live in. Such failures often lead to serious conflicts, and those responsible parties are often referred to as people with low emotional quotients. Therefore, by exploring through reading the emotional conflicts and confrontations experienced by book characters, children can learn to think about the impact of emotions from the perspective of these characters and recognize the various effects that emotions can cause in different situations. Such a learning process is called "empathy training," and it is a very important module in reading education for young children.

Step 4: Let the children learn to control emotions on the basis of understanding them. Picture books often tell stories of someone paying a heavy price for out-of-control emotional responses and how they finally earn forgiveness and regain the balance of life through reflection and apology. Each such story represents a trial-and-error process. Lucky for us, our kids don't need to go through this kind of trial and error in real life. Reading the story with the child with the help of the emotion comparison card is equivalent to letting the child experience the emotional ups and downs of the book characters. As children accumulate more of such empathetic experience, when they encounter similar situations in real life in the future, they will be less likely to lose control of their emotions and be able to better manage their emotions and behaviors.

Step 5: Help children gradually learn ways to master or even manipulate emotions. In addition to allowing children to learn how to control their emotions, using the emotion comparison card can also help children learn to master or even manipulate emotions. Many picture book stories can be used as scripts for acting with emotions, and the emotion comparison card can be used as an auxiliary tool to develop children's performance talents. All great performing artists are actually masters of emotion manipulation. Most of these artists showed a talent for noticing small emotional fluctuations from an early age and finally learned how to express the emotions of the roles they play vividly with facial expressions and body movements. Therefore, in addition to practicing reading with emotions, letting children play a book role with emotions is also good for tapping into our kids' potential performance talents.

※

In the text below, *Angry Arthur*, a picture book, is taken as an example to introduce specific steps of using the emotion comparison card.

Step 1: Preparation of the emotion comparison card through parent-child cooperation. Actually, *Angry Arthur* is not a book that shows many emotions except anger, but it's still OK for the parents to add facial expressions of joy, anger, sadness, panic, and other emotions onto the emotion card.

Step 2: Parents read aloud this "rage-filled" picture book and guide the kid to identify different emotions appearing in it. Looking at the cover first, which shows a little boy named Arthur sitting angrily on the city wall, with a depressed cat lying beside him, parents can ask the child, "What do you think happened to them?" They can also ask their child to point out the emotions of Arthur and the cat on the emotion card and imitate each corresponding facial expression. Then parents can ask the child to think about what Arthur and the cat would want to say. The child is allowed to say something or act as Arthur and the cat. If they are unwilling to do so, parents can give them a demonstration first. Next the family should go to the title page of the book, in which Arthur and the cat appear again, looking angry and frightened, with a lightning bolt slashing beside them as a clear indication of their rage and frustration. At this time, the parent can repeat the steps of emotional identification, which will help strengthen the child's memory. However, if the child doesn't have the patience to repeat and only wants to continue reading, just let them. In each of the remaining pages of the book, different characters appear with various emotions, and the parents can guide their child to repeat the above routine with each of these emotions. In the process of reading, it's very much recommended for the parents to do two things: The first is to guide the child to observe the expressions of Arthur's parents and grandparents when they appear in the story and ask them to identify the corresponding emotions on the emotion card and reenact them; and the second is to remind the child of how the mood of the red cat changes throughout the story and ask them to identify and reenact its every expression, especially a particularly funny one that it has in the scene in which Arthur's anger has brought a tsunami that covers the entire city, and this cat gets to enjoy fishes while hiding behind the chimney.

Step 3: Encourage the child to learn to think from the perspective of others by explaining to them the cause of the emotional conflict and confrontation between the characters of the story. In the case of *Angry Arthur*, emotional conflict and confrontation between characters can be found on pages 1 and 2. In the picture on the first page, we can see that Arthur is watching TV with his mouth wide open, and his expression shows his curiosity, a very common emotion among children; turning to the second page, we can see very obvious emotional conflict as Arthur in the picture is angry and starting to lose his temper because his mother asks him to stop watching TV and go to bed, but we can't see the mother's expression as she only appears as a tall figure projected into Arthur's room. In this case, we can guide the child to imagine how firm and angry the mother's face would be in that situation. Parents can first act as Arthur's mother and show the child the corresponding facial expression, and then switch roles with the child to perform the mother-child conflict in the picture. After the role-playing is completed, the parents can tell the child why the mom and Arthur are angry, so as to let them know where the emotions come from and understand that people should often look at the problem at hand from the perspective of others.

Step 4: Let the child understand the cost of out-of-control emotionis and learn how to manage emotions. In the case of *Angry Arthur*, we can see from page 3 super exaggerated illustrations of Arthur's emotional runaway and how it turns to something that can destroy the entire universe. Reading this picture book will also let the child know how explosive and destructive one's anger can be, to a level so severe that it will have disastrous consequences. In the process of reading, parents can consciously ask the child to recite the lines or perform the scene with emotion, or even compete with the child to act as angry as Arthur in an exaggerated way, so that the child can understand the addictive feeling of the releasing one's anger. We can do parent-child interactive performance based on this picture book's story, which will help discover children's talents in expression and performance.

After his anger destroyed the universe, Arthur sat desperately on the debris of Mars thinking about why he got angry in the first place, but failing to remember any particular reason. Arthur's experience fits the facts as sometimes human emotions can get out of control for no reason. Therefore, we must constantly use the emotion comparison card as a tool to help children discover the independent existence of emotions, recognize emotions, learn how to control them, and eventually become the master of emotions. It can be seen that the emotion comparison card is a reading tool that can really help shape the character of children, which is also one of the biggest features of the graded reading course, which is to promote good character and morals and help children become respectable human beings while helping them learn and fall in love with reading.

Summary

The emotion comparison card is a reading tool that can be prepared in advance of reading a picture book with your child by drawing the expressions of basic emotions such as joy, anger, sadness, and fear on a piece of cardboard. When reading a picture book involving emotional conflicts, we can first use the prepared emotion comparison card to help children understand emotions, then guide them to learn about empathy by reading emotional confrontations and conflicts in the story and finally let them understand the cost of emotional runaway and learn how to control and manage emotions through performance exercises.

Chapter 2

How to Improve Kids' Reading Participation Through Basic Training

Content-repetition approach: How do we use recurring things in a book?

The Content-Repetition Approach

The content-repetition approach means that reading about something over and over again in a picture book helps strengthen a child's memory. When using this method, parents also need to guide their children to find the differences between repeated content, so as to improve their competence in information recognition.

What is the content-repetition approach? Let's start from a certain rule about picture-book content. Parents who are familiar with picture books know that in some picture books certain things reappear over and over again throughout the story, the reason is that such repetition fits the cognitive pattern of children and helps them remember things that are the same or similar. However, content repetition is not just about memory, as parents also need to guide their children to find the differences between repeated things, so as to improve their competence in information recognition.

Brain science tells us that memory is about recording things that happen in life in the human brain and keeping such records so that they can be used when needed, and that memory is required for advanced mental activities such as thinking and imagination. Without effective memory, we can do nothing. For example, many elderly people who suffer from Alzheimer's disease have lost basic living skills because they can't remember things at all. One way to avoid forgetting something is to read about it in books. But how can we remember so much information and not forget it? What are the brain-science principles behind remembering something and freely recalling memory?

First let's do a quick introduction of memory-related brain science principles. Roger Wolcott Sperry, an American brain scientist, conducted a famous experiment that verifies the "left/right brain division theory" about lateral brain function, which earned him the Nobel Prize in Physiology and Medicine in 1981. According to his theory, the brain can be divided into two parts, left hemisphere and right hemisphere. To do anything in life, a human being needs to use both hemispheres at the same time and activate the corresponding brain neurons. However, in terms of specific functions, the left hemisphere is mostly responsible for processing language, text, logic, and analysis, while the right hemisphere is mostly responsible for handling images, sounds, imagination, and creativity. When we need to remember something, we first generate an image of it in the right brain, and then pass the image to the left brain, which converts the image into text information and stores it.

Further brain science research also found that, in terms of memory, our brain works like a bookshelf, where books in different categories are placed in corresponding layers, and each book having its own title and chapters records different information. And our thinking about something is actually a process of translating corresponding memory in the brain into symbols and languages for output.

Then, what's the working principle of the content repetition approach? We all know that reading is a process of taking in knowledge, that is, "getting to know something," and recalling that knowledge for use involves the extraction and integration of stored information, that is, "remembering something." Relatively speaking, the key to true memory is not the storage of information but its extraction and retrieval. To truly memorize a thing, our brain needs to go through the whole process of ingestion, processing, storage, and retrieval of information.

So how can we achieve efficient memory processes? The key to measuring the quality of memory is in the efficiency of extracting relevant information; that is, higher extraction efficiency means more solid memory. Brain scientists have found that the difficulty of storing information in the brain is inversely proportional to the difficulty of extracting the same information; the information that is remembered through hardships is easier to extract, and information that is easier to remember is also easier to forget. It can be seen that the content that is memorized after a lot of repetition can be extracted more easily, and the brain will be more efficient in recalling such content. The content-repetition approach was developed based on the above-mentioned brain science principles; that is, by increasing the difficulty of storing information through high amount of repetitions, we can reduce the difficulty of the subsequent retrieval of such information from the brain. Therefore, for children's reading, the content-repetition approach is an effective tool.

✦

In fact, people started to use content repetition in practice even before the discovery of the above-mentioned brain science principles. Taking a closer look at the long established nursery rhymes and children's poems, you will see that they all contain repeated rhythms and words. Since the creation of these works can be traced back to the early days of human language development, it's clear that people have long known that repetitions can help children achieve effective memory. Similarly, all excellent young children's books also make use of content repetitions in their story line and language rhythm.

In the text below, the picture book *A Dark, Dark Tale* is taken as an example to demonstrate how to use the content-repetition approach to help deepen children's memory.

First ask the child to observe the picture on the book cover, which shows a round window that reveals the head of a black cat hidden in the grass. Next, flip the book to the back cover, which shows a picture of the same window revealing not the head but the back of the same black cat. At this time, you can ask your child what the similarities and differences are between the two pictures.

Letting the child observe the subtle differences between these two similar pictures helps them deepen their impression of the book's theme (dark things).

The theme of dark things is reflected in every picture of this picture book, but each with different settings and characters. You can take the child to observe each picture as a whole first and gradually shift their focus to the details, so as to discover what dark things are in the book.

In the process of reading, you can repeatedly say "A dark, dark . . ." while asking the child to observe how the core scene and order of the animal's appearance changes from page to page, and tell them to find the similarities and differences between every two pages. For example, the first page of the picture book shows a dark, dark wilderness, while the second page shows a dark, dark forest, and both pages feature a total of three kinds of animals: owl, rabbit, and bat; among them, the rabbit appeared twice while each of the other two only appeared once.

Turning to the third page, the picture shows a dark house in which the owl appears again. The next two pages show a dark door and a dark room behind it. There are no animals on these two pages, but there is an animal ornament on the door—a lion head with a big ring in its mouth and a unicorn sculpture in the room. In the pictures that follow, the cat on the cover appeared on a dark, dark stair, then passed through a dark, dark corridor behind the stair and stopped at the corner door, after which it went behind a dark, dark curtain at the end of the corridor. After that, the cat appeared again (with his hind legs and tail exposed) and entered the dark, dark room, at which time he squatted in front of a toy horse and stared out of the picture. We can repeatedly use the "a dark, dark . . ." phrase to describe the above plots while letting the child point out things that are dark in the picture and observe the repetition and change of places, animals, and objects from page to page.

The story of the book reaches its climax at the last few pages, in which the cat first tried to open a dark, dark cabinet in the room and then turned its eyes to a dark, dark corner under the pile of toys in the cabinet, in which there was a dark, dark box. When we turn to the last page, we will see that there is a terrified rat hiding in that box!

Throughout the process of reading this picture book, we can communicate with the child about many things, such as settings, scenes, spaces, animals, objects in the pictures, and use the content-repetition approach many times to help deepen the child's memory and exercise their observation ability. I hope that parents can use this method to help their children understand and memorize the contents of picture books, so as to improve their reading ability and find more fun in reading.

Summary

What are the working principles of the content-repetition approach? The study of brain science tells us that to memorize a thing, our brain needs to go through the whole process of ingestion, processing, storage, and retrieval of information, and that the information that is remembered through hardships is easier to extract, and information that is easier to memorize is also easier to forget. The content-repetition approach was developed based on the above-mentioned principles of brain science. Taking a closer look at the long-established nursery rhymes and children's poems we can see that people started to use content repetition in practice even before the discovery of the brain science principles. In the process of reading picture books, we should guide our children to observe what similarities and differences exist in the pictures and words that appear as the story develops, and communicate with the children from multiple aspects such as place, space, people, animals, objects, etc. as well as asking the children to talk about what they see in the pictures.

Imagination and attention management: How to let children better use their imagination

Imagination and Attention Management

For young children who are new to reading picture books, using imagination and attention management can help keep them focused without imposing unnecessary restrictions on their imagination.

For young kids, paying attention is a basic ability for completing a task, while imagination power determines how much creativity they show in doing that. Both abilities are critical to a child's growth. However, no child has unlimited attention and imagination, and to master both requires continuous learning and development. The human brain follows the law of use and disuse, and for children from three to six years old, the development of brain functions regarding attention and imagination has profound implications for their lifelong growth.

In early childhood education, picture books provide the environment necessary for attention training and imaginative thinking. And for young children who are new to reading picture books, using imagination and attention management can help keep them focused without imposing unnecessary restrictions on their imagination.

The brain of an adult is moving at a high speed when reading, and well-developed reading ability is supported by a complete set of neural network systems for semantic recognition. The reason many adults can read ten lines at one glance and very quickly understand the thoughts or ideas expressed in writing is that they were well-trained in reading-related imagination and attention since early childhood. However, the process of development with respect to attention and imagination differs wildly from one kid to another, which is why many different picture books are created to help us promote said development. However, are there any scientific principles behind such reading-based training?

The latest brain-science research indicates that attention is determined by three functional systems of the brain, namely the attentional orienting system, a primary attention system that develops the earliest; the attention control system, the development of which is the key to improving one's attention focus; and the emotion and reward system, an interactive system that reflects the relationship between children's behaviors and social feedback. We can effectively improve the working efficiency of these three systems by doing reading exercises.

The attentional orienting system, as the first one out of the three systems, starts to develop when a child is three months old, a time by which we often say a baby learns to gaze; that is, when the baby hears something or see things moving in front of their eyes or adults making funny gestures, their attention will be attracted by these external stimuli, which means that the baby's brain is capable of basic attentional orienting. If someone says that a child is smart, if often means the kid can hear and see well, which indicates that their brain is well developed in attentional orienting by hearing and seeing. At the beginning, one's attention highly depends on the auditory and visual systems. We were born with the ability to receive sound and image information (meaning it's part of our innate intelligence). However, when facing a large amount of sound or image information, the brain needs to determine which to store and process, and such a selection function involves attentional orienting, the training of which is of critical importance.

If a child is exposed to high-intensity stimuli and interference from electronic devices such as mobile phones, iPads, and televisions from an early age, their ability to obtain and filter basic information will decline, and they will be less responsive to conventional stimuli. If such a situation continues, it is very easy for the child to get distracted when reading books and attending classes in the future. Therefore, it is very important to keep in mind that parents should guide young children to do reading training based on seeing and hearing, and they should not let children play with electronic devices early on.

The second system (for attention control) is the key to one's self-control as attention itself means how well one can control their own will. Children from three to six years old are very suitable for self-control training, especially those at five, as they can already concentrate for five to ten minutes; that is, even if they are not very interested in something, children reaching this age can control themselves to do only this thing for five to ten minutes.

So, for a child from three to six years old, we can spend from five to ten minutes reading them a picture book, immersing them in the story. In this way we also get to see how the children's attention system is developed. If you find that your child has a rather short attention span, you can choose a simpler picture book to shorten the reading time. After that, you can slowly increase the reading time and difficulty, allowing your child to gradually obtain the proper ability to control themselves.

The third system (the emotion and reward system) is a behavior feedback (reward) mechanism that's mainly responsible for two functions: emotional perception and excitement. For example, if a child is inattentive in class, it may not be because they can't understand the class content or the teacher is doing a bad job, but that they feel that they can't get any meaningful rewards from the class; as a result, they lack the necessary excitement and become reluctant to attend the class, which reduces their ability to maintain attention and makes it easy for them to be distracted. Therefore, to get a child's attention, parents need to integrate certain positive rewards into the reading process, because giving interesting rewards encourages the child to focus on reading and learning, and makes them happy while doing so, indicating that the brain section responsible for excitement is working and the child can better control and focus their attention.

Now let's look at the imagination. Different from attention, imagination involves the nervous system matching one thing with another seemingly completely unrelated thing. For example, a child can imagine an elephant's nose as a bridge, or a corncob as a capsule hotel, etc., while almost no adults can think of either. Therefore, for children from three to six years old, we need to find ways to prevent their childish imagination from fading while improving their power of concentration, which would be a most difficult task for parents.

When children's abstract thinking ability improves, especially after they start to recognize words, their ability to mismatch things, which gives them childish imagination power, begins to weaken rapidly. For example, a child who doesn't know the modern English character "1" can think of it as a flat load, a chopstick, a toothpick, or a cucumber, etc., but after knowing that it represents the number 1, the child will remember the connection between it and "1," and in their brain such a connection will be preferred over associating it with something else. If we ask a child who knows the character "1" to imagine what it looks like, instead of unconsciously mismatching other things as before, they will just try to think of similar-shaped items they have seen in life, indicating that they have lost the imagination power they once had. If for about thirty minutes a day you let your child immerse themselves in picture book stories filled with unrestrained or even ridiculous ideas, it will not only allow them to learn to concentrate on reading but also provide them with a space to release their imagination.

✻

In the text below, the picture book *A Taste of the Moon* is taken as an example to introduce how to use picture book reading as a tool to enhance children's imagination as well as their concentration power.

Step 1: Guide the child to focus on the story and connect things appeared in it. To do this, you should guide the kid to first find the core element of the book story, then gradually connect various content related to it to smoothly reconstruct a complete story line. Taking *A Taste of the Moon* as an example. The core element of this picture book is obviously "the moon," and all the tastes described therein come from the animals' imagination of the moon. Therefore, you can first guide your child to pay attention to the moon itself, and then let them understand that many animals in the book want to have a taste of it. At this time, the child's mind starts to connect various elements in a way like "playing a movie." While reading this book, you can start from the scene in which the turtle is climbing to the hillside to catch the moon and let the children pay attention to the rest of the animals according to the order of their appearance (elephants, giraffes, zebras, lions, foxes, monkeys, mice, and finally, the fish). Such a scene-based "movie-playing" process is crucial for keeping your child's attention.

Step 2: Guide the child to think deeper about what they have seen. When reading the book, the child, as well as their parents, should try to use all their senses to experience everything the author describes. After finishing a part of the book, you should take a pause and ask the kid to think about what the little animals saw, heard, tasted, and smelled. Does the moon taste sweet or salty? What's the best taste you can think of? Is this animal relatively large or small? Is it possible for it to get the moon? When going through each page in which an animal appears, you need to let the child imagine what would happen in that scene.

Whether or not your child understands what they read largely determines whether they can really engage in reading. And such understanding is far more than simply recalling the pictures or the words in the book. Parents also need to guide the child to imagine each scene in their head so that they can truly immerse themselves in the story told by the author and understand it more deeply. The story structure of *A Taste of the Moon* is similar to a movie composed of multiple dynamic slides. There are subtle changes between each two pages of the book (the appearance of different animals brings different behaviors and dialogues, with the overall location having only a slight change). When children read this book, they can see all kinds of fresh things appearing in the same location. As such, this book is very suited for starting to teach children how to concentrate when reading.

As children get older, we can begin to consciously accompany them to read transitional picture books (that is, picture books having more text than pictures), during which we should guide our children to learn knowledge from the book while imagining what's described in it (such as volcanic eruption and tsunami, etc.). After reading for a while, tell the child to pause and think about what they just read and encourage them to mobilize all the senses (hearing, vision, smell, taste and feeling) to enrich their imagination about the scene in the book. Through the above process, children will find that they are fully immersed in the book story, and reading becomes as fun as watching their favorite cartoons. The above imagination training can happen simultaneously with attention training. Young children's healthy growth is inseparable from attention and imagination training and how to randomly switch between the two subtly. I hope that parents can use picture book reading as a tool to improve their children's concentration ability and imagination power as well as how to control both appropriately.

Summary

In early-childhood education, picture books provide the environment necessary for attention training and imaginative thinking. We can use reading to effectively improve the working efficiency of a child's attentional orienting system, attention control system, emotions, and reward system. With the improvement of abstract thinking ability, children tend to prefer abstract cognition over the mismatched thinking that supports childish imagination. Immersing children in the infinite space created by picture books helps not only exercise children's attention focus but also release their natural imagination power. When reading a picture book with your child, be sure to first guide them to focus on watching and listening, then encourage them to use multiple senses to feel things described in the story and get a deeper understanding of things observed.

Immersive-reading approach: What should we do when kids can't concentrate on reading?

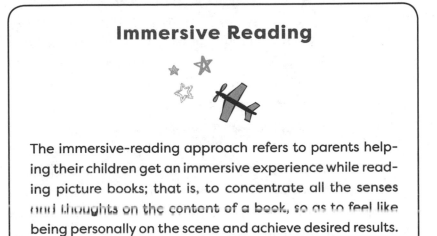

Immersive Reading

The immersive-reading approach refers to parents helping their children get an immersive experience while reading picture books; that is, to concentrate all the senses and thoughts on the content of a book, so as to feel like being personally on the scene and achieve desired results.

If an experience is *immersive*, it is completely surrounded, absorbing, or involving someone, and putting "immersive" before reading, learning, and experience means that corresponding participants are so concentrated on doing or thinking about something that they become completely unaware of all other things in the immediate reality. As a state of mind, immersion represents the highest level of concentration. For example, when a child who is crazy about LEGO blocks is concentrating on building with them, they may even not hear their own name called by someone standing right next to them, in which case we can say that the child has immersed himself in building with LEGO blocks.

Today, the advancement of technology has brought tools that can help people realize immersive reading and learning. For example, AR (augmented-reality) technology that has been widely used for language learning and science learning can make something appear out of a card by scanning it with a mobile phone and that something can actually interact with the real environment displayed in the screen of the phone. VR (virtual reality) is another immersion-inducing technology that has seen widespread use. In many malls and cinemas, VR-based multidimensional entertainment facilities are set up to allow people to experience some immersive sci-fi scenes by putting on VR helmets or glasses. Those who have been to theme parks such as Disneyland or Universal Studios most likely know how exciting and fun these new technologies can be.

Now, these immersion-inducing technologies have been widely used in various teaching scenarios, because both AR and VR technologies can be used to create a near-real virtual learning environments in which learners can achieve skill improvements through highly engaged interactions and exercises. For example, 3D virtual environment-based simulators have been used for flight training and military training. And there are also various immersive learning methods based on games (role-playing games, large game consoles, real-time strategy games, large-scale multiplayer online games, etc.) that have been widely used with great results.

Obviously, higher learning efficiency can be achieved through methods that allow children to directly perceive what they have learned. However, when using ordinary picture books, no available equipment and technology can help us create a simulated virtual environment for children. In this case, we can follow the logic behind the above-mentioned new technologies to help children achieve an immersive experience through picture book reading during the stage of early childhood education, so as to enable the children to read effectively and truly establish a notion about how things in the books associate with those in the real world.

It is repeatedly highlighted in the book *Supercharge a Kid's Brainpower* that the key to early childhood education is to teach children to use all their senses. Current research in brain science has shown that different types of stimuli are processed by different sections of the brain. For example, language and spatial information are processed by the left and right hemispheres, respectively. Based on such findings, it's recommended for parents to remind their children about how the brain works and instruct them to pursue higher efficiency in the daily learning process. For example, when reading and learning something, you can adopt the method of alternating between learning content of different kinds to balance the workload of each brain section, so as to avoid loss of learning efficiency due to excessive use of a particular brain section. Multichannel stimuli input (such as inputs through hearing, seeing, tactile sense, and other sense organs) is also a good way to improve memory efficiency. For example, only 20 percent and 15 percent of things one learns solely through seeing or hearing can be effectively remembered, respectively, while 50 percent of things one learns by both seeing and hearing can be recalled without a problem. We can see that memory efficiency significantly improves when the learning process involves more than one sense.

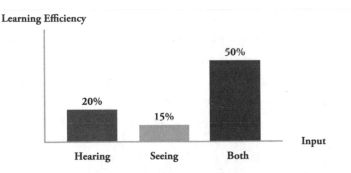

So, in a home environment, what simple methods are available for us to create immersive reading experience and enhance the effect of reading-based early childhood education?

The first method is to teach children to use all their available senses (which may include vision, hearing, taste, touch, and smell). In fact, children rely on sensory input to learn everything. In addition to reading, preschool children should also be encouraged to obtain appropriate stimulus input through various senses in daily lives. The immersive-reading approach can also be applied to children up to age three, but note that children at this stage mainly need to learn how to perform visual tracking, auditory tracking, and obtaining information through their tactile sense. For children aged from three to six, parents need to encourage them to use their imagination so as to have a more diversified immersive reading experience. More important, parents should pay attention to whether the child is really watching and listening during the reading process, and whether they are actually trying to feel something by hand and participate in the interactions. Specifically, when using sensory-based methods to interact with your child, you need to do three things:

Tip 1: Be sure to maintain eye contact with your child when talking to them. By looking at the child's eyes when speaking slowly and keeping eye contact with them, we ensure that the child uses their visual and auditory organs at the same time, so that the dialogue can have a better effect. When talking with children during parent-child reading or other times in daily life (such as playing with toys), we must consciously guide them to look into our eyes or at what we are talking about.

Tip 2: If conditions permit, when reading about some items in the picture book, you can take out the real-world counterparts or samples to let the child get a deeper experience by using all their senses.

For example, when reading about apples or aircraft carriers in a book, you can take out a real apple or a model of an aircraft carrier and let the child observe and explore by themselves, so that they get to know the object through all the senses (hearing, sight, and smell).

Tip 3: Remember that the more senses involved, the better. Looking at a person's eyes when speaking requires the listener to use the two senses of hearing and vision at the same time, while letting the child touch, observe, and smell the apple is to simultaneously call on their three senses. These methods all help a kid to achieve a deeper immersion. For children from three to six years old, parents should pay attention to the training of the imagination. We can describe some scenes orally and let children imagine something from it, which as an extension of and supplement to the picture-book story will help the child get a deeper impression and memory.

With the development of reading ability, children aged from three to six will become more and more sensitive to text and gradually form the habit of reading by only looking.

Based on the theory of multidimensional competition, the advantages of using all senses can be clearly seen: The process of going from 1D to 2D to 3D represents going from a simple line to a shape with multiple faces, and obviously things in 3D are more likely to make you feel immersive. Considering our senses and skills as dimensions, the effect of immersive reading is far better than that of vision-only single-dimensional reading.

The second method is to create opportunities for interaction and an environment that promotes immersive reading. Interaction while reading is also a way to create an immersive experience, because interaction requires children to mobilize at least two senses (visual and auditory) at the same time and to associate what the parents say with the pictures and text they see, therefore helping them to immerse themselves in scenes described in the book. Such interactive reading is equivalent to replaying the book's story line in the brain, which can help children to have a deeper understanding of the story.

With respect to specific interactions in reading, be sure not to only tell the story in chronological and textual order; that is, don't just focus on finishing the story. After reading each section, ask your child a few questions and have a discussion. For example, you can ask your child: Why do the rabbits have long ears and short ears? Why does a turtle have four claws? Why do you think it is black? Why does it go so fast? Why did it fall into the water?

To help children discover the world by reading picture books, we need to ask questions in a step-by-step manner based on the children's interests and thoughts. For example, when the child says "the rabbit's ear was bitten off," you can ask "Who did it and why?" By asking questions according to the children's interests and thoughts, we make reading an interactive game that allows children to interact with their parents and immerse themselves in the story.

Creating an interactive reading environment is one of the least-expensive ways for parents to use the immersive reading tool. By using this method to improve children's reading efficiency and reading ability, we can make them fall in love with reading and develop good reading habits that will aid them in future studying.

Summary

Immersive experience helps children feel like they are personally on the scene and achieve desired reading effects. There are simple ways to create an immersive reading atmosphere in a home environment. The first method is to encourage children to use all their senses (vision, hearing, taste, touch, smell) when reading with parents. When using this method, pay attention to maintaining eye contact with the child or mutual attention to the same thing. When possible, you can take out real-world objects for the child to explore. Just remember that the more senses the child uses, the better the effect. The second method is to use interactive reading to guide children to think and imagine from multiple angles, so as to turn reading into an interactive game that enhances reading efficiency.

The speculation approach: How to make kids more engaged in reading

The Speculation Approach

We are born with narrative and speculative instincts, and the speculation approach refers to using narratives in storybooks to train children's speculative ability in reading.

The speculation approach may sound a little unfamiliar, but most of us should have used it many times when we took English tests in middle school. Among the test questions, in addition to cloze, a typical example for using one's speculative ability, another example that requires some speculation is to select corresponding answers by working out the meaning of the entire text based on picture(s) given. It can be said that the speculation approach is a commonly used reading tool. In some countries that have advanced graded reading systems, you can find very thorough checklists listing what reading skills and reading levels are required for children of different ages. But in China, it's quite common for children to go through early childhood without getting effective reading training. As a result, when these children enter middle school and high school, many of them will find it very difficult to complete reading comprehension questions and cloze questions in English test papers. In addition to insufficient vocabulary, the lack of necessary speculative ability is another reason why they are so weak in answering these test questions.

In fact, all of us are born with narrative and speculative instincts. The latest brain science research confirms that many phenomena of consciousness in human history can be attributed to the narrative needs of the human brain. The cerebral cortex is a part of our brain that first appeared about 200 million years ago, and over a long period of time it has evolved into something that can connect many individual images to form a coherent story line and transmit it to the amygdala. The ability to think may actually be the ability of our brain to associate various kinds of isolated information. The above-mentioned cerebral function lays the foundation of our thinking, and ideas about causality are generated from it. In fact, it's the narrative needs of the brain that drive us to become curious about strange things. To put it plainly, it is because of the inherent narrative needs of the brain that humans want to understand various situations and explore unknown things, which also explains why children like to listen to stories. And speculation approach is a reading tool that helps us train children's speculative ability in reading by using the narratives in book stories.

The brain's narrative needs give birth to a human's speculative ability. Everyone's brain receives various signals from the senses every day. These signals are transmitted to the cerebral cortex, which records and stores them on synapses that connect to neurons. Under normal circumstances, we can call for some information stored in the cerebral cortex when needed. When we recall something, a part of the neurons that store related information become active and start to activate some other auxiliary neurons. For example, when we read some old books with our children, our brain will immediately retrieve the memories related to the book, including its plots and pictures. The above-mentioned recall process is an instinctive reaction, which means that when we see the book, our brain automatically tries to recall its content.

When reading a book for at least the second time, adults often find that they can predict what happens next upon seeing an illustration, while children often turn straight to pages containing the funniest plots. The reason for the above is that after the brain obtains information from the outside world, it compares the information with what is stored in memory and makes predictions based on the results of such comparison. In most cases, the above prediction occurs unconsciously as it represents a kind of cognition that the brain automatically generates after obtaining input information.

Therefore, parents need to use effective enlightenment and training methods to cultivate their children's ability to make predictions when reading, so as to simultaneously activate the children's narrative and predictive instincts and effectively improve their reading ability.

※

The text below introduces some simple ways to apply the speculation approach during reading to improve your child's reading skills.

First of all, don't try to finish the book in one go. Take a pause from time to time and encourage your child to guess what will happen next. In particular, if your kid is aged from three to six, ask them, "Do you know what will happen next?" If they say, "I don't know," you can guide them to take a guess based on the book title, the pictures, and the plots they have already seen by asking, "All right, just try to take a guess. Based on what has happened so far, what do you think would makes sense to happen next?" For example, for a child who has never read the book *Olivia*, you can encourage them to guess what story the book tells based on illustrations in the first few pages. First, you let the child look at the picture carefully to ensure that they can make reasonable guesses. For example, after seeing the picture on the first page of *Olivia*, you can ask the child: "Does Olivia like singing or dancing?" After they give you an answer, you can continue to ask: "What else might Olivia like to do? Do you think she likes to ride a bike, play yo-yo, or do handstands?" In this way, the child can try to make some reasonable assumptions based on the existing clues and their own life experience.

After turning to page 5 of *Olivia* and seeing that Olivia is angry with her brother because he has been following her, we can ask the child: "Why is Olivia getting angry with her brother? Does she not like him?" so as to encourage them to speculate, prompting them to pay more attention to book content and complete the reading process with greater concentration. After making predictions, children will be more eager to know about the subsequent story line because they want to verify whether their predictions are correct. In this case, their interest and participation in reading will naturally improve. Moreover, the process of speculation also trains children's advanced thinking skills, such as inferential ability and imagination.

Second, when reading, parents should pay attention to communication and interaction with their children, that is, to make timely feedback on their children's reading performance. After the child obtains certain reading skills, you can teach them to use gestures (such as raising one and two fingers) to indicate that they can or can't understand the book content. If the child uses gestures to indicate that they do not understand, you should stop and read the page again or guide them to look at the illustration carefully and help them understand the story.

Knowing when you don't understand is actually a very important ability that requires whole-brain linkage. The reason why some children repeatedly make the same mistakes when doing homework after school is because they have not learned to monitor whether they really understand the questions so they just mechanically copy the correct answers. Similar problems can also occur in reading, especially for children who have obtained certain reading skills that enable them to repeat a lot of content as they often unconsciously choose to just complete the reading task without confirming whether they understand what they are reading. Letting children use gestures to indicate they understand or not is equivalent to introducing a upper-brain-based monitoring system that enables children to measure by themselves whether they really understand the content. Many kindergartens in the United States let children between the ages of four and five learn this self-monitoring method. However, it should be noted that many children may not fully understand this method at first, in which case the parents should be patient and take it slowly as their kids may just not be ready for it yet.

Summary

We are born with a narrative instinct in our brain that promotes us to tell and hear stories. And it's natural for our brain to make predictions by comparing old and new information. As such, in reading sessions parents can intentionally ask their children to predict what happens next, including taking a pause from time to time and encouraging the child to take a bold guess about what will happen next based on the book title, the pictures, and the plots already seen. Also, parents should pay attention to the communication and interaction with their children when reading, so as to provide timely feedback on their children's reading performance and help them monitor if they really understand the content of the book.

Chapter 3
How to Improve Kids' Reading Concentration and Consistency

Plot-connection approach: Why kids forget what they just read

Plot Connection

The key to the plot-connection approach is that logically connected and coherent story lines are easier to remember. Regular use of this method in parent-child reading with young kids promotes the creation of a virtuous cycle of reading enjoyment and deeper memory, which is conducive to improving children's interest and ability in reading independently.

For adults, plot connection is a most basic reading skill. However, young children are more accustomed to divergent thinking. For them, it's easy to think of outer space when looking at any picture book but rather difficult to find by logical thinking some seemingly simple associations and linear connections. Rich imagination is certainly not a bad thing, but children still need to learn how to identify connections and continuity in a narrative; that is, neither imagination nor linear thinking should be developed at the expense of the other. Patricia Bauer, a well-known American child psychologist, has conducted a study on childhood memory loss, especially how and why some things that were originally remembered during childhood are forgotten by us over time. Childhood memory loss is closely linked to the plot-connection approach described in this section for the following reasons.

Let's start with a brain science experiment conducted by Patricia Bauer. In the experiment, the research team recorded some three-year-old children's daily life activities with their parents, including family trips, parties, and visits to the playground and the zoo. After a few years, when the children became a little older, the researchers conducted tests on whether they could remember the events recorded, and the result showed that many things had been forgotten. Specifically, the research team found that these children could remember about 50 percent of the recorded events when they were five or six years old, but that number dropped to around 30 percent when they reached the age of seven to ten. Seeing such results, the researchers developed a strong interest in things that had not been forgotten and what kind of things are more likely to leave a strong impression. After doing some comparison research, the researchers found that things that can leave a deep impression on children's brains can be mainly divided into the following three categories:

The first category covers events involving greater emotional ups and downs. Events that brought great joy or pain to a child, such as being scared to the point of crying by horror movie scenes, or bad dogs, or stumbling badly on the road when distracted by someone, tend to leave strong impressions in the child's mind and are more difficult to forget. Even many adults can remember some of the most frustrating experiences or the happiest moments of their childhood. However, most of what children read until the age of six can't leave an impression as strong as such events above. Only after the children reach the age of seven and learn how to read autonomously will they remember by repetition some reading materials that they found particularly interesting, but this kind of autonomous learning is beyond the scope of early childhood education.

The second category includes logically connected and coherent story lines, which reflect the key mechanism by which the plot-connection approach works. Considering the mutually reinforcing relationship between memory and logical reasoning, it's easy to understand why kids tend to remember stories featuring clear causality and close connections between details, and why content with awkward expressions and far-fetched connections will soon be forgotten by children. As such, it's recommended for parents to make regular use of the plot-connection approach in parent-child reading with young kids, which will promote the creation of a virtuous cycle of reading enjoyment and deeper memory and help improve the children's interest and ability in reading independently. For example, asking your child to keep a logical and organized account of what happened when writing a diary will help improve their basic reading and writing skills.

The third category covers nursery rhymes children often listen to and sing. Based on the basic principles of the content repetition approach described earlier, it should be easy to understand why children can remember those included in this category.

By looking at Patricia Bauer's psychological experiment, it can be found that those events that bring emotional stimulation can't be planned and it is difficult to integrate them into young children's reading education. However, the plot-connection approach and content-repetition approach are two methods that can be applied in parent-child reading. Moreover, the psychological mechanisms underlying the plot-connection approach tell us that this method is critical to children's reading efficiency.

❋

In the text below, the picture book *Harry the Dirty Dog* from our graded reading list is used as an example to show you how to use the plot-connection approach. The picture book tells the story of a puppy who doesn't like taking a bath, which starts with the puppy going out to play and getting so dirty that even his family couldn't recognize him, and ends with him taking a bath after knowing the consequences of not doing it.

In this book, we can find that every two pictures are connected and what happens on each page can promote plot development. In other words, this book tells us a complete story through closely related pictures and plots, and the puppy in the story represents a child who likes to play but hates bathing. When reading the book, you can guide your child to pay attention to the color of the dog and the bath brush that serves as an important prop, so as to use them as clues to connect the plots of the story. The first page of the picture book tells us that Harry, a white dog who was afraid of taking a bath and had black speckles on his body, ran away with a bath brush in his mouth. The second page tells us that Harry secretly buried the bath brush in the backyard. From the third page, we can see how Harry turned himself from a white dog to a "black dog," including making half of his body black by playing at a road construction site; turning the whole body gray-black by playing on railway tracks; blacking his whole body by playing hide-and-seek with other dogs in the grass; and finally, turning into a "bright black" dog by sliding up and down on a coal conveyor belt . . .

In reading the above plots, you should guide the child to observe how the color of the puppy changes from page to page.

The remaining pages of the picture book tell us that the puppy was hungry and ran home, but the family did not know such a "black dog" at all. In this case, Harry had to go to the backyard to get the bathing brush and ask his family to give him a bath. After the bath, Harry became himself and returned to the arms of his family. And in the end, Harry secretly hid his bath brush under the blanket he was sleeping in.

The book's story line features both smooth progress and brilliant plot reversal, making it worthwhile for parents to read with their children repeatedly. In addition to deepening children's memories of the plot connections, repeated reading of this book is also good for exercising children's ability to tell stories and helping them practice how to understand unfamiliar content based on illustrations.

During the reading process, you can keep asking your child questions such as: "What did the puppy do just now, and what color was his body in the previous picture? What is he doing now? Why does he look somewhat different than before?" Use these questions to guide your child to look at the picture carefully and think about how the plots on every two pages are connected, so as to help them find the main clues that drive the plot. Because there is only one main character, the story in this book is more coherent. You should repeatedly ask your child to confirm clues behind plot development by asking questions such as "Where did the puppy play?" "What happened there?" "What happened later?" The purpose of such questions is to guide the child to pay attention to the change of the puppy's body color and deepen their impression of corresponding plot development. After finishing the book, you can show the child two pictures on the front and back covers, one featuring a clean Harry, and the other Harry the Dirty Dog, so as to let the child reflect on what caused such obvious color difference. Such a systematic review of the story line can help the child remember key points of the story.

I hope that parents can use this method to help continuously deepen children's effective memory obtained by reading, and help them learn to find the basic plot connections and how to coherently tell a complete story line. In this way, children will gradually master the skills of information extraction and obtain higher self-confidence in completing reading tasks, and eventually gain the ability to read autonomously.

Summary

Logically connected and coherent story lines are easier to remember, while content with awkward expressions and far-fetched connections will soon be forgotten by children. In the process of parent-child reading, parents should pay attention to guiding children to discover the connections between plots on every two pages and help them find the main clues that drive the development of the story. After reading a book, parents should ask their children to conduct a systematic review of the story and connect all plots based on the main story line. This will help the children learn how to extract key information from a storybook.

Ritual-of-reading approach: How to inspire respect for reading

The Ritual of Reading

We need to establish a ritual of reading with our children at home, which means doing parent-child reading at a fixed time and place to minimize unwanted interruptions or disruptions. This approach helps children develop a respect for reading and become better at it in terms of self-control, time management, and learning efficiency.

When it comes to rituals, many people may immediately think of ancient witchcraft, myths, or some religious activities. Fei Xiaotong, a famous sociologist, stated in the book *Hometown China* that: "Rituals, including most ancient religious activities and acts of worship at later times, play an important role in cultural heritage." In life, we all have to go through various rituals, including those for festivals, weddings, funerals, and national ceremonies. It can be said that rituals have penetrated into all aspects of human life. But what do rituals have to do with graded reading for young children? In other words, why does the sense of ritual help children develop an interest in reading and the ability to read autonomously?

More than one hundred years ago, Arnold van Gennep, a famous French anthropologist, proposed that rituals are things we always do upon the transition from "one scene of life to another" for the purpose of acquiring specific feelings and emotions.

As the most important way for people to understand themselves, others, and the world, reading plays a very crucial role in one's self-development. For this reason, we should consider the activity of reading to be as important as daily behaviors such as eating and drinking. In order for the entire family to truly value reading, we need to find ways to identify reading as an important thing that is different from daily activities. To do this, we need to do parent-child reading at a fixed time and place to minimize unwanted interruptions or disruptions, so as to help children develop a respect for reading and become better at it in terms of self-control, time management, and learning efficiency.

Someone may find it hard to believe that the sense of ritual can really help children achieve so many goals. In fact, by studying the sense of ritual from the perspective of psychology and brain science we can understand why it is so amazing.

The latest brain-science research shows that human autonomy comes from self-esteem and that one's ability, consciousness, willingness, and motivation will be greatly improved when self-esteem reaches a state that is different from or better than normal. Establishing a sense of ritual is a way to make people feel different from normal.

Next, from a psychological perspective, rituals represent deliberate adjustments of environment for the purpose of making it more in line with inner expression and self-esteem. It is not difficult to find that having a sense of ritual means that one wants to strengthen certain inner speech and establish certain spiritual "sacred moments" by changing the external environment. Based on the above principles, in the field of early childhood reading education, strengthening self-esteem by establishing a sense of ritual means making children realize that reading is a higher-level activity different from normal activities by clearly defining related states of mind and behavior.

Reading often in a solemn and awe-inspiring atmosphere would leave a strong psychological impression in the child's mind that reading is an important activity. In this case, every time a child starts reading, they will unconsciously adjust their reaction, mind readiness, and concentration to a higher level in preparation for this important activity. The aforementioned development pattern is in line with the positive-reinforcement theory proposed by American psychologist B. F. Skinner: Pleasant results gained from a certain behavior will in turn push people to repeat said behavior. In other words, the praise and affirmation that children receive for active reading behaviors will motivate them to read more. As such, we can see how ritual of reading can inspire a respect for reading and motivate children to learn more by themselves.

In real life, some parents do not value the sense of ritual, deem it as something of no practical value, and ignore it. Under the influence of such a mindset, these parents tend to casually deal with many important events in life, never thinking to create a sense of ritual for reading, which often causes them to get further and further away from an excellent life. However, according to the aforementioned findings in brain science and psychology, any sense of ritual, even one created by simple on-the-spot arrangements, can still help us achieve higher self-control and action efficiency.

It can be said that all rituals come from important wishes and certain needs of human beings. Reading reflects people's desire and need for knowledge, and by enhancing the sense of ritual in parent-child reading at home, we can help our children better satisfy their need and desire for more knowledge and experience as well as self-development. The psychological suggestion brought by the sense of ritual will subtly transform into a desire for knowledge deep inside the children's minds. It is often said in daily life that one should "work only when he believes in it sincerely" or "remain true to the original aspiration," both of which reflect the strong needs and motivations that promote us to do certain things and realize certain wishes to the best of our ability. Well, we can create such needs and motivations by means of self-suggestion brought about by the sense of ritual, and reading often in a solemn and awe-inspiring atmosphere will help children receive more of such beneficial self-suggestions.

*

However, many families do not have or value the ritual of reading, especially that of reading picture books for young children. What can we do to make ritual of reading an important part of life? Here are a few suggestions:

Suggestion 1: The whole family should get together and reach a clear consensus on why we want to read because finding a clear motivation is a prerequisite for creating the ritual of reading. Without clearly understanding the role of reading in promoting children's growth or letting your child truly realize the benefits of reading, you can't establish a truly effective ritual of reading, no matter how hard you try otherwise.

Suggestion 2: Set a fixed area and time for parent-child reading. Parents are advised to establish a reading corner or any area dedicated to reading (sofa, desk, floor or bed) when the child is still a baby, and always read with their child at one or more fixed time periods every morning, afternoon, or before bedtime. One important reason why some children find it hard to read consistently is that their normal reading process is often interrupted or disrupted. However, it's only normal to have such interruption and interference because most parents overestimate their children's willpower. In fact, even adults may not always be able to insist on doing something meaningful for a long time, and it's only natural for children to give in to the temptation of instant satisfactions (such as snacking, watching TV or playing games). As such, in order to effectively block out such temptations, it's necessary to set a dedicated time and area for reading. The reason why themed summer camps and short-term closed trainings tend to yield good results is that the activities of these programs are carried out at fixed places and times, in which case the participating children will unconsciously be better prepared in mind and body—the exact result we want to achieve by taking the ritual-of-reading approach.

Suggestion 3: Make standing rules with the child for the regulation of actions and thoughts during reading. It is recommended to write on a piece of paper or a piece of cardboard the commitments to reading and behaviors that are not allowed during reading (such as snacking, finger picking, and nail biting). The process of writing these rules is by no means redundant, because it represents one's emphasis on reading. After all, the core purpose of the ritual-of-reading approach is still to let children learn and fall in love with reading. In other words, making standing rules is to express and strengthen personal awareness and to create a prerequisite for compliance. After making the rules, you should emphasize the importance of following the rules and keeping promises to your child. During the reading process, the child may violate the rules, in which case you must point out each violation and have them correct their behavior. Over time, the child will eventually form the habit of abiding by the rules while reading.

Many of us may remember that in the famous children's book *The Little Prince*, there is a dialogue between the prince and a fox about the sense of ritual.

"It would have been better to come back at the same hour," said the fox. "If, for example, you come at four o'clock in the afternoon, then at three o'clock I shall begin to be happy. I shall feel happier and happier as the hour advances. At four o'clock, I shall already be worrying and jumping about. I shall show you how happy I am! But if you come at just any time, I shall never know at what hour my heart is to be ready to greet you. . . . One must observe the proper rites."

"What is a rite?" asked the little prince.

"Those also are actions too often neglected," said the fox. "They are what make one day different from other days, one hour from other hours."

Summary

The sense of ritual is about strengthening self-suggestion by changing the external environment, and taking the ritual-of-reading approach in early childhood reading education means clearly defining reading as an activity more important than normal daily behaviors. Reading often in a solemn and awe-inspiring atmosphere would leave a strong psychological impression in the child's mind that reading is an important activity. In this case, every time a child starts reading, they will unconsciously adjust their reaction, mind readiness, and concentration to a higher level in preparation for this important activity. It's recommended to do three things when taking the ritual-of-reading approach: **1.** To get together and reach a clear consensus on why we want to read; **2.** To set a fixed area and time for parent-child reading, and **3.** To write down the commitments to reading.

Stepped lead-in reading:
Does word-by-word reading really help?

Stepped Lead-In Reading

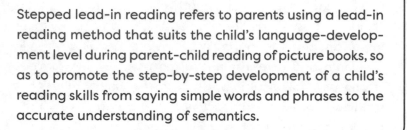

Stepped lead-in reading refers to parents using a lead-in reading method that suits the child's language-development level during parent-child reading of picture books, so as to promote the step-by-step development of a child's reading skills from saying simple words and phrases to the accurate understanding of semantics.

The stepped lead-in reading mentioned in this section actually refers to the parents of children aged from three to six using lead-in reading methods that suit the children's language-development levels during parent-child reading, so as to promote the step-by-step development of the children's reading skills from saying simple words and phrases to the accurate understanding of semantics. Taking stepped lead-in reading helps the parents avoid two common pitfalls in leading in reading.

The first pitfall is reduplication abuse. For children aged up to three, parents often use words of reduplication—such as choo-choo, night-night, bye-bye, wee-wee, poo-poo—during daily communication and parent-child reading, thinking that this method can deepen the children's memory and encourage them to express themselves. In the Baby Bear picture book series, a very popular set of young children's books, there is one book titled *Poo-Poo* that is particularly well received among children. Under the subjective notion that reduplication is good for communicating with children, some parents stick to using it for a prolonged period of time. Of course, for a certain period of time, using reduplication is actually consistent with the principles of cognitive science. For children under the age of two, who are yet to master enough vocabulary and language skills and find it difficult to understand normal conversations between adults, using reduplication is good for teaching basic expressions and common sense, because words of reduplication sound more intimate and are easier to understand and repeat. However, such positive effects are time-limited. For children over two years old, continuing to use reduplication on a daily basis will have an adverse effect on the development of their language competence.

The second pitfall is finger-reading. When it comes to parent-child reading, some parents like to use finger-reading to tell stories to their kids and encourage them to read. The "finger-reading" mentioned here refers to reading text word by word to the kids while pointing a finger to each of the words and slowly stressing each syllable, which would make a sentence like "This is a cow" sound like four separate sentences: "This. Is. A. Cow." We can see that this method makes us sound like bad artificial intelligence tools. It has a seriously adverse effect on the development of children's vocabulary and semantic understanding ability.

Children's language development is actually the process of mastering language knowledge in order from easy to difficult (from words to phrases to sentences). Parents should try to maintain standard pronunciation and clear and moderate speech during parent-child reading but never cut a sentence into separate words. For children from three to six years old, parents should choose lead-in reading methods appropriate for their kids, so as to guide them to walk on the correct path of language development. Remember, to promote the development of a child's language and reading skills, the best way is to let them gradually learn how to communicate as the adults do.

⁂

Research in brain science shows that, rather than the general belief that the abilities that support children's language and reading competence are listening, speaking, reading, and writing, it actually comes from the parts of the cerebral cortex that are responsible for processing different components of the linguistic system (phonology, vocabulary, semantics, syntax, etc.). In this case, instead of guiding children to read based on the so-called four-ability system (listening, speaking, reading, and writing), we need to carry out graded reading education in accordance with the scientific laws behind reading and language development.

Language development starts from one's birth. For babies, the voice of adults speaking represents valid language input, and upon reaching six months old, they can start to repeat simple spoken words. From this point on, under the constant stimulation of language input, neurons in the corresponding brain regions become more and more active. And it's actually the activation of auditory system neurons (including those on the upper temporal lobe) that leads to a baby's babbling. At the same time, the "myelin" outside the neurons also begins to develop, which helps to solidify the simple language skills a baby has acquired.

At the age of eight months old, babies begin to recognize simple vocabulary on their own. After that point, infants develop a variety of abilities that can be used to distinguish between various prosodic structures. After learning to recognize the frequency of words based on certain statistical rules, the baby's brain gradually develops the functions needed for distinguishing the meaning of words. In other words, an eight-month-old baby can distinguish between words and phrases that appear in a two-minute conversation and know which of those words appear repeatedly in said conversation.

Beginning at the age of three, children acquire more-mature semantic-discrimination capabilities. As such, still using word-by-word reading would be counterproductive to their understanding of the words and sentences. Therefore, for three- to six-year-old children, it's no longer appropriate to use either reduplication or finger-reading, which may hinder children's understanding of spoken words and semantics.

✦

As the language competence of children aged from three to six develops very quickly, their parents need to help them master the basic units of language in the right way and learn how to understand and organize more-complex language structures based on these basic units. Cognitive linguists believe that it is the above structure that constitutes the language knowledge system, and that such a system remains in a dynamic state. Based on the foregoing findings, this chapter makes the following three suggestions.

We need to gradually reduce the frequency of using reduplication in picture-book reading. To help children understand and recognize normal spoken language, reduplication should be completely removed from reading when a child reaches three years old.

Second, don't read word by word during the parent-child reading process, but take a pause after reading semantically complete sentences continuously, in which way we can gradually improve the children's ability to understand the phrases and whole sentences formed by words. It should be noted that reading too fast is also not good, otherwise the child might make hearing mistakes. Some parents may ask, "Can I use fingers to guide my child to read?" It's OK if the child has already developed an interest in the words. Just remember to point your finger to the last word in a sentence and read said sentence to the child in one go. For example, you can point to the last word "buffalo" in the sentence "This is a strong buffalo," and repeatedly guide your child to read this sentence.

Finally, you should consciously exercise your child's language comprehension at different levels while repeatedly reading the content of a picture book. For example, on the first go you can put your finger on the last word of a complete sentence and read the sentence continuously. On the second go, you can swipe your finger across the entire sentence to be read and guide the child to read and try to understand the whole sentence or just repeat after you. In the above process, you should encourage the kid to imitate and speak out, and to read more than one word in the sentence together by asking: "Great, you already know these words. Let's do it again and see if you can read them together!" This approach helps develop the child's reading and comprehension skills in a step-by-step manner (from words to phrases to whole sentences).

Summary

Children's language development is actually the process of mastering language knowledge in order from easy to difficult (from words to phrases to sentences). For children from three to six years old, parents should choose lead-in reading methods appropriate for their kids, so as to guide them to walk on the correct path of language development. As the main influences on a child, parents should try to maintain standard pronunciation and clear and moderate speech during parent-child reading. After the child is three years old, parents should ditch all reduplications, otherwise it may hinder the child's understanding of normal speech. The best way for parents to improve children's language and reading skills is to help their children learn how to communicate as adults do. When reading picture books, parents can consciously encourage children to imitate and speak out and help them gradually learn conjunctions and sentences, so as to continuously improve their competency in reading and understanding.

Phased-targeting approach: How to make reading as addictive as playing games

Phased Targeting

Phased targeting refers to breaking up a general objective about reading into smaller individual tasks, so as to form a framework of progressive advancement. In essence, the phased-targeting approach should be about helping children develop good reading habits and self-discipline by means of goal management and instant motivation.

In a literal sense, phased targeting means breaking up a general objective into smaller individual tasks, so as to form a framework for progressive advancement. However, such a definition does not reflect the essence of phased targeting in graded reading, as simply breaking a big goal into smaller ones won't really help children fall in love with reading. Parents who regard reading as a task imply that it's something mandatory and purposeful. Nobody likes to be forced to do something, and reading is no exception. As a result, just setting reading tasks, phased or not, would be meaningless or even counterproductive.

Really effective phased targeting means using instant rewards to make children gradually fall in love with reading or even become "addicted" to it. You might ask, reading is so different from watching TV or playing games, how could someone be "addicted" to it? The "addiction" mentioned here refers only to a brain activity mechanism that causes people to be very enthusiastic about something. If we can combine the principles of this mechanism with an appropriate goal management strategy, it's entirely possible to "design" a "ladder" that leads to one's love for reading. What is the brain activity mechanism that makes us love something?

It's common knowledge that dopamine is a nerve-conducting substance. From the 1980s, for a long time, the scientific community believed that dopamine was the key substance in the brain that induces the feeling of happiness and excitement.

However, the above long-held consensus in the scientific community was overthrown by the findings of Kent Berridge, a neuroscientist from the University of Michigan. Kent discovered through experiments that while normal wild mice enjoy the sight of their favorite food, increasing the expression quantity of dopamine in them by 70 percent doesn't make them any happier, only more active in seeking food, indicating that dopamine does not induce the sense of pleasure, but only the desire to obtain it. It's a wonder how the brain works, right?

As a result, the brain science community has reached a new consensus that desire and happiness belong to two different systems, and while dopamine can induce the former to make people tirelessly pursue something; the latter can be defined as a feeling of satisfaction and is not directly related to dopamine. In other words, under the action of dopamine, we may want to pursue something that we don't actually need or like; that is, we are "addicted" to it, but actually getting this thing does not make us happier. We need to know more about how to make children really enjoy reading instead of being simply "addicted" to it.

The latest brain science research shows that in the process of a behavior becoming a habit, the brain section activated by said behavior gradually shifts to the impulse-triggering "corpus striatum." In other words, when a certain behavior becomes a habit, it's less susceptible to the control by the "prefrontal cortex" responsible for rational reflection. Habitual addiction represents an unconscious behavior, and "addiction" represents an imbalance between impulse and rational thinking. Dopamine-induced "addiction" to bad behavior is purely impulsive, and it's difficult to quit because said "addiction" is less susceptible to rational control. However, if we can somehow make children "addicted" to knowledge-seeking and reading, it should have a positive impact on their learning and growth.

We know that making a decision requires the simultaneous activation of two brain sections, the striatum and the prefrontal cortex. The former is the self-reward center responsible for generating impulses, and the latter the rational-thinking center responsible for controlling impulses and measuring consequences. In other words, the striatum works like an accelerator that promotes one into action, and the "prefrontal cortex" acts like the brake system. The interaction between them determines a person's level of decision-making skill and self-control.

The self-reward mechanism (impulse system) in the brain of a child from three to six years old is rather primitive and more susceptible to strong stimulants (such as animation or mobile games) that promote the release of dopamine, and such dopamine will then further enhance the child's desire for said stimulants. The self-control mechanism (reflection system) in the brain of a three- to six-year-old child is also immature, making it less effective against the aforementioned "addiction."

Many parents use material rewards to encourage their children to read and learn. But scientific research indicates that once such material rewards are removed, the child's self-reward mechanism will become even more active, while the self-control mechanism in their brain becomes less active. If the material reward stops, the child will give up reading and learning and find something else (such as games and cartoons) to do that will bring them instant satisfaction.

Based on the above, when reading picture books for young children, it's recommended that parents highlight by encouragement or other means the sense of enjoyment brought by reading itself. It should be noted that the encouragement mentioned here does not include empty compliments such as, "You are so smart, so awesome," because the key to such encouragement is to give positive feedback on the child's specific behavior. For example, saying, "We've finished another book, and you listened very carefully just now; I'm so proud of you," will give the kid a clear indication on what they did well, which will then promote them to repeat the same behavior.

There are many other ways to reward children, including spiritual rewards, such as encouraging, affirming, appreciating, and admiring the child's growth; emotional rewards, such as smiling, hugging, clapping, touching, and high fives; and activity rewards, such as traveling with parents and playing games with other children. However, for children, the best reward is actually allowing them to freely choose one thing that they like to do. For example, after the child has independently read a book and completely recounted the story in the book, or after they performed well in a great "family story party," you can allow them to choose to either play with their friends for a while or watch some of their favorite cartoons.

The key to phased targeting is to make completing reading goals as fun as clearing game levels. In other words, parents should act as the "game designers" and set instant rewards for completing each task, which will promote dopamine secretion and make the children more willing to continue!

There are two key points to note when using the phased-targeting approach:

The first is timetable and checklist, which acts similar to what a progress bar does in a game. Parents of younger children can work with their children to develop a daily reading list and teach the children to manage by themselves what, how much, and when to read each day. Of course, it's not necessary to only list reading tasks in a timetable, because the timetable can also contain necessary daily actions such as drinking and sleeping. Making timetables and checklists allow children to understand when and what should be done, which is conductive to the development of a clear concept of time.

The second is instant reward. Pay attention to setting rewards according to the schedule, such as giving children a corresponding number of tokens or credits when they complete tasks on time, which can be used to exchange for some of their favorite material rewards. The word "instant" mentioned here mainly emphasizes that children should be rewarded immediately after completing the task. Of course, in addition to material rewards, there are many other forms of rewards, and you can choose to use any one or a combination of them according to specific circumstances.

In essence, taking the phased-targeting approach in parent-child reading is to cultivate good reading habits and self-discipline in children through goal management and instant motivation mechanisms. As the old saying goes, "freedom comes from self-discipline." Only developing children's goal-management and self-discipline ability from an early age will make it truly possible for them to enjoy free reading without the intervention of their parents.

Summary

The self-reward mechanism in a child's brain is rather primitive and more susceptible to strong stimulants (such as animation or mobile games) that promote the release of dopamine, which will then further enhance the child's desire for said stimulants. To make the matter worse, the self-control mechanism in a child's brain is also immature, making it less effective against the aforementioned "addiction." Note that when material rewards used to encourage good performance are removed, the child's self-reward mechanism will become even more active, while the self-control mechanism in their brain becomes less active. Taking the phased-targeting approach requires the parents to develop with their kid a timetable covering both daily reading tasks and corresponding instant rewards (including emotional rewards, spiritual rewards, and activity rewards). The rewards will be given to child immediately after they complete a task in the timetable.

Chapter 4

How to Develop Good Reading Habits

Word-locking approach: Can preschool children learn to recognize words?

The Word-Locking Approach

In simple terms, the word-locking approach refers to guiding kids to first know the story through pictures and then find words they already know from the text. The purpose of this is to help children learn to understand the meaning of words and the connection between words and pictures.

As a reading training method commonly used in early childhood reading education, the word-locking approach is designed to help children learn to understand the meaning of words and the connection between words and pictures by guiding them to first know the story through pictures and then find words they already know from the text.

This seemingly simple method can lay the foundation for the development of reading ability. To understand the reasoning behind such a statement we need to first know about the term "word blindness."

There is a boy named Percy, who was very smart and energetic during early childhood, as good as any of his peers. Percy started to attend school at the age of seven, and showed no IQ or vision problems. He encountered no obstacles in mathematics learning. In addition to recognizing individual Arabic numbers, he could easily learn more complex numbers and even understand mathematical formulas such as $(\alpha + \chi)(\alpha-\chi) = \alpha2-\chi2$. However, Percy encountered great obstacles in learning to read, even struggling to spell monosyllables at the age of fourteen. The teacher went to great lengths to help him learn to read, but all efforts failed, and text seemed to be an insurmountable obstacle for Percy. Later, a doctor declared after diagnosis that Percy has word blindness. Percy possesses the intellectual and perceptive abilities necessary for reading, but is unable to read written text, indicating a deficiency related to the comprehension of letters and words. Percy can easily recognize the Arabic number 7, but not the word "seven." Now we know that Percy is suffering from developmental dyslexia.

Percy's story tells us that knowing and understanding words lays the foundation for all reading comprehension. Doctors have also found that some adults who had no problem reading may experience acquired dyslexia after brain trauma, which means they can see the words but can't understand the semantics. We can see that it is impossible for a child to acquire autonomous reading ability without learning to understand words.

The most important meaning of the word-locking approach described in this section is that for preschool children, the first step in learning to read is to understand words, the basic units of all texts. With the continuous improvement of relevant abilities, children will become more and more interested in written words. After accumulating enough vocabulary, children will be able to get a lot of information through reading. Therefore, the word-locking approach is very suitable for the reading education of preschool children, and, after using this method, parents will find that their children's reading ability has been improving without them noticing.

✦

In the text below, the book *Make Way for Ducklings* is taken as an example to demonstrate how to use the word-locking approach to help children improve their reading skills. *Make Way for Ducklings* features some long sentences, so it is more suitable for four- to six-year-olds and less so for three-year-olds. Information density and sentence length are the basic indicators to consider when deciding whether a book is suitable for children.

After getting the book, you should first have an overview of the story with your child and then guide them to find the words they already know on each page, which will be the focus in subsequent learning. At this time, you can write such words on a piece of paper or make a list of them in a certain order and paste the list on the wall so that the child can remember the words through constant review. Although we do not encourage some old-school word teaching, the fact remains that without knowing the words, children will never be able to read freely on their own because they can only understand the story by looking at pictures.

Which words should we focus on? It's recommended to choose words based on the answers to the following four questions (still using *Make Way for Ducklings* as an example).

Question 1: Does the word affect one's understanding of the story? Children must learn all the words that are important for the story. The way to test whether a word is important is to delete it from the text and see if the child can still understand the story without issues. Taking *Make Way for Ducklings* as an example, the word "place" appears many times in the book as it represents the shelter the duck family has been looking for; that is, the home for the family. It can be seen that removing the word "place" from the text will make it difficult for the child to understand the story in this picture book. In this case, we need to focus on learning this word by guiding the child to guess its meaning based on the context of the story.

Question 2: Does the child use this word autonomously? As parents, we also have to learn to observe and record which words our children use in their daily lives. After finding a word important for the book story, you should check whether your child uses it in daily activities (when playing games and communicating with peers). Obviously, children from four to six years old can already say "this place" and "that place," but they may not know the word "place" in written form. In this case, you need to remind the child how and when the word is used in their daily life, teach them its meaning, and help them associate the meaning of this word with its written form.

Question 3: Does the word frequently appear in different contexts? It helps children to remember the meaning of a word when it is repeatedly used and reviewed in a large number of different scenarios. In view of this, parents should pay attention and remind their children of words that appear repeatedly in various texts, so that children can gradually grasp its various meanings. When introducing a new word for the first time, parents can choose to only introduce its simplest definition, such as "'place' means any area set aside for a particular purpose." After finishing a book, parents can provide different definitions of the word in different contexts. For example, "place" can mean "a point located with respect to surface features of some region," as in "this is a nice place for a picnic," or "an abstract mental location," as in "a place in my heart," or "a general vicinity," as in "He comes from a place near Chicago."

Understanding a word can enrich your child's language system while improving their ability to understand texts and stories. After the child is familiar with a word, you can ask them to point out pictures related to this word in the book they read or guide them to use this word or other elements related to its meaning by asking some questions while reading. Only doing such multiple reviews can make children truly grasp what a word means. However, it should be noted that the aforementioned activities should be performed only after the reading process is completed, otherwise they may affect the coherence of reading and the child's overall understanding of the story.

Question 4: Does this word relate to other words the child is learning? The connection with other words being learned is good for the child's understanding of a new word. With this in mind, we can see that parents' preparation before reading is crucial and only parents who know their child well can make the right choice. For example, when reading *Make Way for Ducklings*, if you know beforehand that this book contains some abstract words, such as "proud," "responsibility," "calling," "commitment," and that your child can understand the word "tasks," you can tell your kid when reading something that involves "responsibility" that "responsibility" and "task" can be used together in a sentence like "You have responsibility for this task." If you know that the child may not understand a word, you can stop and explain the meaning of the word in detail with the words the child has already learned, or ask the child to guess the meaning of the new word before explaining. The latter method also helps the child understand the meaning of words based on context and represents an important way to improve children's autonomous reading ability.

The word-locking approach is suitable for use in most picture books with more texts and longer stories, which are mainly designed for children four to six years old. You can make good use of this method in training your kid's basic reading skills.

Summary

Knowing and understanding words lays the foundation for all reading comprehension, and it is impossible for a child to acquire autonomous reading ability without learning the meanings of words. Taking the word-locking approach means that, after getting a book, you should have an overview of the story with your child and then guide them to find the words they already know on each page, which will be the focus in subsequent learning. It's recommended to choose words to be focused on based on the answers to the following four questions: **1.** Does the word affect one's understanding of the story? **2.** Does the child use this word autonomously? **3.** Does the word frequently appear in different contexts? **4.** Does this word relate to other words that the child is learning?

Family story party:
How to motivate kids to read more

Family Story Party

A family story party is the gathering of all family members to tell stories to each other. Storytelling is an active output process that requires the use of oral expression and language organization, which also is good for improving children's cognitive competence.

When it comes to the family story party, we need to focus on two keywords: "party" and "story." The word "party" means that all family members are involved in the activity, and that everyone, including the child, must tell a story and not just listen to one. It can be said that to throw a really effective family story party, the most important thing is that children must be truly involved in the storytelling process. The other keyword, "story," is equally important, because storytelling is different from gossiping or chitchatting, as most stories are fictional. Telling a good story requires the narrator to be good at imagination, language organization, public expression, and creating conflicts and surprises. Based on the above, we can see that why "party" and "story" are the two most important things to keep in mind when throwing a family story party.

The text below presents an analysis from the perspective of the two keywords on why the family story party is very conducive to enhancing children's reading and thinking skills as well as personal growth.

First, let's analyze the matter from the "party" perspective. In traditional parent-child reading, parents are always the narrators and children the listeners, representing a passive pattern that has little effect on improving the children's expressive ability. Of course, it is undeniable that children can also have fun and other gains by just listening to stories, but they need to do much more according to the requirements of graded reading education, because the purpose of graded reading is to comprehensively improve children's reading abilities, including the ability to receive and transmit information. Therefore, if a child is always just "listening to" and "looking at" picture-book stories, their development in reading competency would be greatly limited.

We all know that children learn to understand themselves, society, and the world by listening to stories and reading and that cognitive ability is directly related to one's view of life, the world, and values. When a child grows up to be an adult with the above-mentioned "Three Views," they will be able to influence the world around them through what they say or do, which depend on what they transmit to the world. In fact, a person's information-output capacity largely determines their influence on the outside world. Other than determining a child's influence on the outside world in the future, does information-output ability affect a child's life at the moment?

Of course it does, and its effect can be most directly reflected in the entrance tests for kindergartens and elementary schools. At present, high-quality kindergartens or elementary schools all set ever-stricter entry requirements. During the admission tests of these organizations, many teachers will ask children to tell stories, including sharing their favorite stories and telling stories based on pictures, indicating that these organizations value children's ability to tell stories. As such, when taking the time to read picture books with our children and telling them the stories, we might as well exercise their ability to tell stories. The family story party represents the best way to carry out such training, because it allows children to fully express themselves and release their imagination through storytelling, therefore improving through practice their oral expression and language organization.

Beginning in elementary school, children will need to improve their ability to write stories by exercises in picture writing or regular writing. To write a story, one must know how to tell the story first, and the family story party provides the best stage to train a child's storytelling skills.

Catherine E. Snow, an educational psychologist at Harvard University, has found through research that children who could tell stories before the age of six tend to perform better in learning and social interactions in elementary school. Through psychology and research in brain science, we find that when telling stories, children need to make comprehensive use of vocabulary, language organization skill, imagination, and memory as well as moral judgment and life experience, all of which have a significant impact on the development of cognitive abilities and therefore a profound impact on children's growth.

The second key word in "family story party" is "story" which is also a key element that promotes the transition from "ordinary brain" to "reading brain." In addition, every story also demonstrates interaction between innumerable elements. Large-scale reading did not appear until the invention of modern printing technology in the fifteenth century, which means that widespread reading has only a history of a little more than six hundred years. Before reading became popular, humans mainly relied on hearing and looking at real objects to obtain information. It can be seen that the human brain is not born ready for reading, and to transform it into a truly efficient "reading brain" requires more than ten years of progressive training with graded reading materials organized according to scientific laws. "Graded Reading on Good Character and Scholarship" was introduced for just the purpose of helping children achieve such a great "brain transition."

Other than reshaping one's cognition, graded reading training can even change the physiological structure of the human brain. In a brain science study, children with and without education from families with similar social and economic status were selected to receive brain scans, and the results showed that the corpus callosum of an educated child is thicker than that of an uneducated child. The corpus callosum serves as a bridge connecting the left and right brains, and its work efficiency determines the speed of information exchange between both hemispheres.

Brain scientists also found through experiments that in the occipital-temporal area on the left side of the brain of those with better reading ability, there is a brain area dedicated to processing text information, which is given the name "text brain section." In addition to processing text information, this "text brain section" can also act as a router that transmits and distributes text information. Taking the idiom of "quenching one's thirst by thinking of plums" as an example, people can do such a thing not because they can image the taste of plums out of the blue, but that when they see the word "plums," the "text brain section" works to translate the abstract text into the intuitive perception of plums. Better reading ability means the "text brain section" is more efficient, and the function of this brain section largely determines a person's ability to "tell a story."

If we think of the brain as a parking lot, then in a normal brain, because there are no rules, many vehicles are parked randomly, and the flow of vehicles in and out of the parking lot is completely out of order. In the "parking lot," vision, language, attention, memor,y and other brain systems are like painted lines, parking spaces, railings, and passageways. In a normal brain, these systems have not been integrated into a complete framework, so they cannot cooperate with each other. However, by doing reading activities, especially reading and telling stories, we are injecting a logical flow of information to the brain the same as setting the rules for the orderly collaboration of the systems in the "parking lot." With such rules, the components of the "parking lot" now can collaborate with each other in an orderly fashion, and such collaboration will continue to improve over time, representing the continuous improvement of human intelligence. However, compared with improving personal intelligence, the impact of storytelling ability on group collaboration has a far more profound significance.

In his book *Sapiens: A Brief History of Humankind,* Yuval Noah Harari uses the term "cognitive revolution" to describe the great influence of language on human beings. The advent of language allows people to form more cohesive groups (including tribes and nations) and execute more complex plans, as well as giving humans the ability to tell stories. The reason why humans can become the rulers of the earth today is because humans can tell fictional stories, which is a capability that other species do not have. And this capability is what makes it possible for humans to collaborate in the pursuit of some nonphysical elements such as "value," "mission," and "vision" on a scope far more widely than that of cooperation in and among other species. It can be said that lack of storytelling ability will reduce the ability of a child to collaborate with others and such a reduction can, in turn, limit what they can achieve in the future. Please keep in mind the above so that you understand how important the "family story party" is to a child.

＊

The family story party is indeed good for improving children's storytelling ability, but it seems rather complicated, so what needs to be done in practice?

It is not difficult to apply this method, as you only need to keep in mind that the most important thing is to let the children really participate in the activity, including asking them to portray a character in the picture-book story. Taking *Duck on a Bike* as an example, after reading the story, you can encourage your child to portray the duckling, while other family members take on other roles, such as the cow, the sheep, and the cat, and then play out the story through the joint effort of the whole family. By giving a vivid performance, you can stimulate the child's desire to participate, making them more willing to remember the plot and dialogue of the story. After the child is familiar with what the duck says in the book, parents can switch roles with them so that they can experience portraying the cow, the sheep, and the cat in the story. The above training process can greatly improve the child's ability to tell the picture-book story independently. If the child does not like role-playing, you can also design a simple interactive game to reproduce the scene in the picture book with the child. For example, you can let a child have a cycle race with a duck doll by riding a toy bicycle, which would greatly increase the child's interest in participating in and retelling the story.

Participation is the key to the effect of a family story party, and such a connection is supported by corresponding scientific principles. Brain scientists have found that the sense of participation stems from the oxytocin released in the brain and the simultaneous excitement and sweat secretion when we receive trust or friendly treatment from others, which work to encourage us to respond to the aforementioned trust and friendship. These findings reveal three key connected elements of storytelling: Attention, connection, and action. Attention means concentration, and it's easy to understand why storytelling requires concentration. However, no one has unlimited attention, and we will only focus on those things that seem important. Stories that don't attract our attention will not lead to effective information transmission, making it impossible to trigger connection and subsequent action (participation in storytelling). Now we understand why good stories can attract children's attention and lead to positive actions.

Most picture books with interesting plots and more than two characters can be used as acting scripts in a family story party to train children's ability to tell stories. I hope parents can make good use of this method to quickly improve their children's reading and expression skills.

Summary

Parents need to know that family story party has two key principles, which are to involve children in the storytelling process and to ask kids to tell fictional and imagined stories. Telling a good story requires the narrator to be good at imagination, language organization, public expression, and creating conflicts and surprises. For children, storytelling has many benefits, including helping them perform better in entrance tests for kindergartens and elementary schools in the near future and improving their intelligence level and contributions to group collaboration in the long term. When throwing a family story party, remember to let the children really participate in a family performance that reproduces a vivid picture-book story with more than two characters.

Alternate reading: How to nail knowledge in children's minds

Alternate Reading

Alternate reading aims to improve the diversity of children's reading materials. Parents may provide children with picture books of various topics, such as stories about humans, animals, or popular science. Otherwise, after reading through a book, children may first carefully reread its third part and then move back to its first part, thus to read alternately.

"Alternate" means to alternate between two or more types of content. Alternate reading means to improve the diversity of children's reading materials in a period when they are three to six years old. Parents may provide their children with picture books about popular science, about animals, and about humans. Otherwise, children can first read the third part of a book and then go back to its first part. This kind of alternate reading may produce good reading effects beyond developing the imagination. Many parents believe that ideal reading and learning must follow rules, move step-by-step, and focus on the same content. However, this is actually a serious misunderstanding of our brains.

Peter C. Brown, a management consultant, has sorted out the views of dozen authoritative cognitive psychologists in the world over the years, and drawn a set of new conclusions about how our brains learn and perceive the world. He finds that distributed training and alternate practice work better than deliberate and massed practice. This new cognitive theory shows how we can make children reap better learning outcomes through effective reading practice. It is necessary to gain more knowledge about alternate reading, which plays a strong guiding role in reading enlightenment and learning achievement.

Many people have heard of the ten-thousand-hour law. It means that to become a master in a certain field, you must spend at least ten thousand hours in deliberate practice about that field. However, there are actually some flaws in this theory. New research has proven that only repeating deliberate practice cannot result in becoming a true expert. A cognitive psychologist conducted an experiment on the training of sandbag shooting. The test required the children of Group A to compete against Group B to shoot a sandbag into the basket three meters away. They were divided into two groups. Group A always stood three meters from the basket to practice. This is deliberate practice. Group B stood two meters away for a while and then four meters away, but never three meters away, for practice. After a period of practice, the two groups were asked to enter a contest for higher shooting rate. The results came as a big surprise. Group B, which practiced by never standing three meters from the basket, had a much higher shooting rate than Group A, who always stood three meters away. This phenomenon is quite jaw-dropping. The psychologists later found, through research, that shooting requires understanding of three-dimensional space. Actually, a basketball cannot always be in the same plane with the real court. The world around us is three-dimensional, so deliberate practice in the same plane cannot solve the problems in a complex three-dimensional world. Living in the three-dimensional world, we need to set up a comprehensive knowledge network by integrating separate knowledge.

Therefore, psychologists have provided new insights into the learning effects of deliberate practice. To be specific, repeated reading and massed practice result in inefficient learning; while distributed, alternated, and diversified learning methods, combined with continuous deliberate practice, are truly effective. Why is this happening? In fact, brain scientists currently believe that the essence of learning is determined by knowledge chains and memory knots. If the human brain is compared to a pearl necklace and what we have learned to pearls, learning is like the process of beading a pearl necklace. Repeated reading is like repeatedly stringing pearls at one end of a thin chain without stopping them from dropping at the other end. Similarly, we cannot remember content that we have only repeatedly read. This is called repeat deliberate practice, and it is noneffective. Then, how can we keep pearls on a necklace? Memory knots! Tying a knot on the chain can stop the pearls from dropping. How to tie this knot? In other words, how to make reading or learning truly effective? Alternate reading is one of the solutions.

How can parents perform alternate reading in the process of parent-child reading? There are three methods for reading practice.

First, distributed-reading practice. Before moving to specific procedures, let's see a psychological experiment where the psychologists tested the efficiency of intern doctors in learning how to perform an operation. The first step is to teach them how to connect small blood vessels through surgery. Second, the interns were divided into two groups. Group A intensively learned the four parts of the surgical procedures in a few days, and then returned to their normal work. Group B adopted the mode of distributed learning. They learned the first part in the first week and then went back to work, and similarly the second part in the second week, the third part in the third week, and the fourth part in the fourth week. One month later, the psychologists tested the learning effects of the two groups by examining how long it takes them to finish an operation, the times their hands had moved, and the success rate of reconnecting blood vessels. The results showed that the performance of Group B with distributed practice was much better than that of Group A with massed learning. It also attested that memorizing and learning require a process of "knotting" the knowledge chain.

Similar methods can be applied to the reading of picture books. We should let children alternately read different picture books, instead of reading only the same book. Picture books can be classified into several categories, such as animal stories, including the *Mole and the Baby Bird*, and *The Rhinoceros Horn of Sudan*, and human stories, including *Miss Rumphius*, *Last Stop on Market Street*, and *Titch*. Parents may read picture books of different types, so that their children can experience distributed-reading practice, which has better results.

Second, alternative-reading practice. The first method emphasizes time intervals, and this method underlines order adjustment. For example, when learning something that has four steps, we generally learn each step in order. We first practice and master the first step, and then move to the second step, and so on. This is a step-by-step learning method but not effective enough. Brain scientists and cognitive psychologists reckon that alternative practice works better. It means learning the first step, then the third step, and then the second step. It seems to take longer than step-by-step learning. However, it produces better results than step-by-step learning in terms of mastering knowledge and retaining long-term memory. It is because alternative practice helps develop our ability to identify different issues and select proper tools among more and more solutions.

We can also employ this method in reading picture books. First, skim through a book and divide it into three parts for detailed reading. Then, read the first part, followed by the third part and finally the second part. Alternative reading may make it harder for children to understand a book in a short time, but it can effectively enhance children's ability to understand and memorize complex content in the long term.

Third, diversified-reading practice. The emphasis of this method is on the diversity of the degrees of learning difficulty. The previous example of sandbag shooting showed that diversified practice can improve learning efficiency. If we always read simple books for children, they may be happy. However, this kind of simple intensive practice has limited reading and learning effects. Reading diverse and more-difficult picture books requires more intellectual effort, but it can strengthen children's reading and understanding skills. The knowledge learned by children in this way will be turned into a more flexible troubleshooting ability by their brains and can be applied in a wider range of situations.

Besides, it would be better to combine tests with alternate reading. At a school in Columbia, Illinois, scientists arranged an experiment where two groups of children would learn some simple scientific knowledge with different methods. The children in Group

A adopted the old method of learning under the guidance of their teachers without any tests. The children in Group B needed to take quizzes about the knowledge they learned. In a unified examination one month later, the students in Group B who had quizzes to test their knowledge averaged A–, and the average grade of Group A, who had no such quizzes, was C+. Why there was such a big difference? It is because taking quizzes can help children retrieve information. If children can actively retrieve information during reading and learning, better learning and reading habits will be formed.

Summary

Learning is like stringing pearls on a necklace. Repeated learning is like unceasingly beading at one end without preventing the pearls from dropping at the other end. To keep pearls on the necklace, the method of alternate learning is a must to tie a memory knot on the "learning chain."

Parents can divide picture books into different categories and read them alternately for their children, so that their children can experience distributed-reading practice.

Parents can also employ alternative-reading practice when reading picture books by dividing a picture book into three parts and reading the first part, then the third part, and finally the second part. With this method, children's ability to understand and memorize complicated content can be effectively improved.

Parents should provide their children with picture books of various degrees of difficulty. More-difficult books may consume more brainpower, but the process of reading them can effectively enhance children's ability to read and understand varied material.

Reciting fluently:
What are the benefits of reading aloud?

Reciting Fluently

Reciting means to read certain words loudly and clearly. The method of reciting fluently refers to the children carefully listening to recitation and gradually participating in it under the guidance of an adult. It can keep children's brains in good shape through the movement of mouth muscles and the tongue and improvements in airflow.

In recent years, both public schools and various educational institutions have been emphasizing education in reading aloud. It seems easy to recite, just reading words clearly and loudly with various verbal meanings. In fact, recitation has some hidden relation to brain development, which explains why the poems we recited in our childhood remain fresh in our memory.

We know that listening to parents reciting is good for developing the children's reading ability. Some parents think it is a waste of time to recite to children because of their children's poor understanding. But it is not the case. When children are listening to their parents reciting picture books, their language and understanding skills are improved unconsciously. Researchers at the University of Illinois surveyed and studied 205 children who have strong reading comprehension. The results showed that these children were basically able to read on their own before starting school. What they have in common is that a habit of reciting and reading has been developed at a very early stage.

The difference between reciting and reading is whether any sound is made. Reciting is a process of changing written words into sound where several organs participate, including the eyes, ears, and the vocal system. It involves aspects of rhythm, meter, imagery, and emotion. It is necessary for the effective training of children's brains. Brain scientists have confirmed, through lots of experiments, that reciting can promote the healthy development and growth of the temporal cortex. The cortex in the right brain is responsible for identifying and expressing rhythms. Some brain-science researchers conducted a targeted training in terms of rhythm, recitation, and music for children with disorders of temporal lobe development. Three months later, NMRIs of that part of the brain showed different degrees of improvement of the physiological functions. A research institute on brain science in California found that children fond of reading and singing or rhythmic exercise can better control their emotions than ordinary children. They also have better thinking ability and language comprehension.

Parents can continuously promote children's brain development by reciting nursery rhymes to children up to three years old and enlightenment materials to children from the age of three to six. During daily guided reading, we can read picture books loudly for children, recite poems with them, and have some rhythmic exercise together. By doing so, we can improve not only children's multisensory abilities but also their comprehensive reading abilities.

The method of reciting fluently is also called "brain yoga" in the field of graded reading. Under the guidance of parents, the children concentrate on what their parents read or gradually begin to recite with their parents. In this process, their brains, especially the frontal, temporal, and parietal lobes, can be activated by the muscular movement of their mouths and tongues. Reciting can also balance cortical inhibition and excitability and keep blood flow and the regulation of neural functions in a good state. As the ability to recite fluently develops, children's brains will also become more alert, as a result of which their memory and attention will improve.

＊

Reciting is not only a method of reading enlightenment but also has other significance and functions. It carries the love of parents to their children.

Jim Trelease, an American educator and the author of the bestseller *The Read-Aloud Handbook*, suggested that parents start reciting stories to children as early as possible. "When did you start talking to your children? On the day they were born? If your children are old enough to understand what you say, they may also understand what you read." He advised parents to "find time to read aloud to your children no matter how busy you are." In his opinion, it is the best gift that parents can give to their children other than a hug.

Jim Trelease and his wife have read as many books for their two children as the number of meals eaten by their children. His own interest in reading also comes from the good habit he formed in childhood. His parents often read to him, which laid a good foundation for his success and the classic *The Read-Aloud Handbook*.

The daughter of Mark Thomas was born with a cognitive disorder. As inspired by the book, Mark and his wife stuck to reciting to their daughter every day without interruption. Even when she was undergoing a surgery, they asked the nurse to play the recorded reading. Their efforts paid off later. When their daughter was five years old, she was able to read on her own. She is very fond of reading, and her literacy was praised by her teachers as "incredible." Scientists concluded that reading-aloud education plays a positive role in early reading enlightenment to shape children's behaviors. As children grow up, they will regard the sound of reciting as a sound that makes them feel safe.

The mother of the former US President George W. Bush also urged parents to read aloud to their children. She said "I always try to recite as much as possible with my children, and sometimes I also ask them to read to me. Some of them are still used to reading with me after growing up. When they are on vacation or free, we will take turns to read a classic. Sometimes we will have a discussion on brilliant parts." In addition, Barbara Bush also used many other methods to improve her children's interest in reading. For example, the family chose a favorite children's author at set intervals, then each member of the family performed a famous story by that writer. This is how to combine fluent recitation with family storytelling parties to enlighten children about reading.

Reciting is not only a tool of reading enlightenment but also an effective method of developing brains and improving learning efficiency. Reciting can excite the brains of children and stimulate them to deeply understand the content of picture books. Children need to concentrate and "empty" their minds of irrelevant thoughts when reciting. Reciting can also improve their memorizing efficiency. The process of reciting can help children open their brain circuits from surface memory to deep memory, making their memory more enduring. In fact, there is lots of preloaded genetic information in children's right brains. Reciting fluently can activate their ability to retrieve that information for life. As children grow older, they will have a deeper understanding of this power and thus improve their quality of life.

Reciting is not only a tool of reading enlightenment, but also helps children master complex words or stories. After children can read on their own, if the parents or teachers continue to recite to them, they will hear some complex words or stories they cannot grasp on their own. It helps them to gain the background knowledge of various topics. Parents should note that reciting doesn't mean to only read bedtime stories. Any written materials, as long as they are suitable, can be recited to children at any time. For example, when seeing street signs and ads on the streets, parents can read them aloud and ask their children to repeat. Parents can read newspapers and picture books that can be seen everywhere in daily life to their children. Any materials in which their children show much interest can be read aloud.

Reciting is not only a tool of reading enlightenment but also shapes the personalities of children. The evolutionary history of humans shows it is precisely because of the development and enrichment of language that the functions of human brains have been developed and improved, allowing humans to become the wisest of all creatures. Reciting can make children more confident and help them to overcome the psychological barriers of being too introverted. Introverted children can't, don't want to, or aren't good at using language. However, under the active guidance of parents, they can learn to read aloud with relaxed muscles, power articulation, measured tones, and strong emotions. They can also express their courage, strength, feelings, and understanding by reading aloud. Then, the children will become more extroverted and have a more integrated personality. An extroverted and communicative child will achieve greater success.

Now that we have learned that reciting has so many benefits, what should we do to help children read aloud fluently? There are thirteen authoritative suggestions for parents on how to recite. They were put forward by Trelease, in his *The Read-Aloud Handbook*.

1. Start reciting as early as possible and keep on doing it till your children finish primary school.

2. Find time to do things that you think important. Schedule at least one fixed reading time each day to help your children develop the habit of reading.

3. Begin with rhythmic nursery rhymes, children's songs, and picture books with a few lines of characters, make the transition to children's books with more words and fewer pictures, and then move to stories and novels with several chapters.

4. Recite to your children as often as time permits. But don't keep it too long in case they lose interest. Gradually increase the time.

5. Avoid reading long descriptive sentences and paragraphs, unless your children's imagination and attention are good enough. Make proper reductions or deletions. Parents may read through the book to mark such long sentences.

6. If a chapter is very long, or you don't have enough time to finish a chapter in one day, stop at a suspenseful point to make your children look forward to the next part.

7. Give your children several minutes to settle down and find a comfortable posture and proper mood to listen to stories. Before moving to a new part of the same book, ask your children where you stopped yesterday. Emotion is an important factor when listening. "Stop now, keep quiet, sit up,

and listen carefully." Such a compulsory tone cannot create a good atmosphere for listening.

8. After a story is finished, leave some time to have a discussion with your children and let them explore the story. Help them express their feelings by speaking, writing, or other means. The key is to do this in a manner that your children like. Don't let the discussion become a quiz, and never compel them to explain the story.

9. The most common mistake, for readers of seven or forty years old, is to recite too fast. Reciting slowly allows children to outline images in their minds. If parents read aloud with a slower pace, their children can watch the pictures in the book carefully. A reader can't use the skills of expression if reading too fast.

10. Find answers together with your children by referring to reference books or handbooks if they have any questions about what you read. It can widen their knowledge and develop their skills in using library resources.

11. Mark the beautiful articles and sentences that are worth memorizing with a little star. One of the ways for children to interact with the books they read is to write notes at the wonderful parts.

12. It is generally difficult for children with ADHD or a reading disorder to sit down to listen carefully. Paper, crayons, or pencils can make them busy while listening. (Adults also doodle when taking a phone call.)

13. The best way to make your children stay focused for a longer time is to spend separate time with each child. This has many advantages for reading stories to children and paying attention to their reactions.

There are some other notes for parents based on the author's research and experience.

First, choose proper picture books for children according to their ages. Second, read to children at a relatively fixed place and time and avoid being interrupted by other factors. Third, parents should first learn to recite rhythmically and emotionally and then they can inspire their children's desire to read. Fourth, if your children ask you to recite the same content several times, don't refuse them because of repetition. Fifth, try to explain the story first and then read it aloud, so that children can have a chance to participate. Sixth, make some mistakes on purpose to test if your children pay any attention to what you read.

Summary

Reciting is to change texts into sound. In this process, many sensory organs, such as the visual, auditory, and vocal systems, are involved, and many aspects such as rhythm, meter, imagery, and emotion are concerned. It is a necessary process to effectively train the brains of children.

Reciting is not only a tool of reading enlightenment but also has other signficance and functions. It represents the love of parents for their children. It can effectively develop children's brains and improve their learning efficiency. It can help children master complex words or stories and shape an integrated personality.

Chapter 5
Training Children's Basic Reading Ability

Role play: What is children's true understanding of books?

Role Play

Role play means children and their family members play the roles in a picture book or story, so as to understand the essence and beauty of the book through immersive performance. Children can feel the emotions of these roles, and start a magical journey with them.

It can improve children's understanding abilities and reading skills.

We have mentioned role play in the context of the family story party as an action plan for the party. In this section, we will further analyze the principles of role play and systematically introduce how to use it.

Role play is a very important reading strategy in the early reading education of children from three to six years old. Moreover, role play is widely used for group learning in English classes in primary school. Therefore, laying a good foundation before school can make it easier for children to learn role play in the future. In fact, role play is one of the most basic learning methods. Let's have a look at the underlying reasons.

On the surface, children have a role-play game with their families, friends, and classmates by each acting as a character in a picture book or story, so role play can improve children's understanding and reading abilities by involving them more deeply in stories. In fact, it is much more complicated. The essence of role play is imitation, which is the key ability for human learning and cultural development. To explain the brain science mechanism of imitation, we should start with a kind of mysterious nerve cell in our brains.

In 1996, Giacomo Rizzolatti, a brain scientist at the University of Parma, and his research team discovered a special type of brain cells, called mirror neurons, in the brains of monkeys. These cells are stimulated when a monkey does actions by itself or when it sees other monkeys doing similar actions. Later research further proved that these mirror neurons also exist in human brains and allow humans to feel others' emotions, such as joy, fear, anger, sadness, and disgust. For example, the same kind of nerve cells will be activated when someone smells a rotten egg and when he/she sees another person smelling a rotten egg and showing strong disgust. In other words, when we see other people's expressions or emotions, our mirror neurons will be activated to let us experience their feelings and emotions.

Then, what is the relationship between mirror neurons and imitation? Rizzolatti, the discoverer of mirror neurons, believes that mirror neurons are the basis of imitation, and that it is the ability of detailed imitation that has shaped human civilization. About 75,000 to 100,000 years ago, human civilization experienced a great boom. During that period, humans invented clothing, tools, and early arts and religions. The brain capacity of ancients much earlier was actually no less than that of modern humans. Then, why did human civilization thrive in that period? According to Rizzolatti, mirror neurons came into being as result of a genetic mutation in our brains. After that, the imitation ability of humans become more powerful. The ability of detailed imitation, the most powerful tool, was then used in cultural transmission, technological advancement, and interpersonal understanding. Humans rely on mirror neurons to learn new knowledge and interact with others, because our cognitive and imitation abilities are based on the functions of mirror neurons. Mirror neurons in human brains are characterized by visual thinking and intuition. They are of great significance for understanding the origin of humans' ability to think and the evolution of human culture.

The main functions of mirror neurons are as follows:

First, mirror neurons can help us quickly understand the intentions of others. Mirror neurons are the basis of imitating other people's actions and learning and are the bridge of human communication and connections in all aspects. Mirror neurons are very similar to the neural circuits that store memories in our brains. They also have their own shortcut keys in that behavioral habits can be quickly formed. Thanks to these characteristics, we can make basic actions without thinking and immediately understand without undergoing a complex reasoning process when others make these actions. If a person's entire mirror-neuron system is destroyed, their cognitive ability will be so reduced that they can't respond to stimuli.

Second, mirror neurons can help us better experience the emotions of others. When trying to understand the emotions of others, the observer can directly feel their emotions, because the mirror mechanism can generate similar feelings in their own brain. In other words, the observer experiences the same neurophysiological response as the observed, thus creating direct experiential understanding. For example, sometimes yawning, sneezing, and laughing are infectious. This is because of the functions of mirror neurons.

Third, mirror neurons can help us build a good language foundation. Patricia Marks Greenfield, a psychologist at the University of California, said in a study: "Mirror neurons provide a strong biological basis for the development and evolution of culture. Mirror neurons can directly absorb culture. Every generation educates the next generation through imitation and observation." Michael A. Arbib, a neuroscientist at the University of Southern California, said that human language is based on mirror neurons. According to Professor Arbib, complex gestures and the movement of the tongue and lips of humans when they speak are based on the same principles.

*

The role-play reading tool introduced in this section aims to improve children's reading and learning abilities by corresponding action plans and the functions of mirror neurons. To be specific, based on the advantages of picture books and children's interest in them, parents guide their children to read a picture book and help them understand the characters, plots, essence, and beauty of the book through immersive role play. Role play allows children to participate in a story, follow the plots, and experience the emotions of the characters in the story, so that they can put themselves in the story and start an amazing journey with those characters. It can promote the development of children's various abilities.

What should parents do to make a good use of role play, so as to improve their children's reading and learning abilities? There are three steps.

Step 1: Recognizing and understanding the characters. Parents guide their children to recognize the characters in a picture book. This is the first step for guiding children to read a picture book with the method of role play. However, it is not enough to just tell them, "This is a puppy, and that is a kitten." We should help our children understand these characters and their feelings more deeply. We need to guide them more specifically. For example, guide them to watch the pictures carefully and use several reading methods to help them understand the plot. Thus, our children can perform the story more vividly and brilliantly by role play.

Step 2: Become familiar with the lines of the characters. In this step, parents practice the lines of relevant characters with their children by using different reading methods and helping their children perceive the changes of these lines and how the plots were driven by these lines. Thus, children can better understand the lines and plots, laying a good foundation for the next step.

Step 3: Encourage children to show themselves freely. The essence of the relationship between "reading and acting" is "feel—imitate—express." Role play based on the reading of picture books is not only the extension of basic reading but also of in-depth reading, and an immersive training in learning and expression. Role-play activities are carried out based on children's understanding of the stories in picture books. Role play is a method of "expression," so children's overall feelings about a story should be demonstrated in it.

How can the method of role play be used in school teaching in addition to early reading enlightenment? Role play is often used for group learning in school. Children can form interest groups in class to discuss or enact the stories or other things they have learned. They must carefully and independently read what they need to discuss or play before the formal role play begins. Next, they should choose a character they can or want to play according to their own interest. Choosing characters autonomously can give children a chance to find and strengthen their potential and make them feel a sense of responsibility and mission.

The role play in school teaching is much more complicated than that carried out in a family. It can train and improve children's ability to learn cooperatively, make each student perform their duties with a clear sense of responsibility, and encourage them to use multiple methods to analyze picture books or literary works from various perspectives. In the process of autonomous role selection, children gradually learn how to coordinate various relationships within a group and how to listen to various arguments and opinions. This is a comprehensive training process, which is very beneficial to the growth of children.

Summary

The essence of role play is imitation. Mirror neurons are the basis of imitation.

These neurons can help us quickly understand the intentions of others, feel their emotions, and lay a good foundation for language.

There are three role-play steps to improve children's reading and learning abilities.

Step 1, guide children to recognize and understand the characters; **step 2,** help them become familiar with the lines of relevant characters; and, **step 3,** encourage them to show themselves freely.

Q&A games: How to cultivate children's ability to think independently

Q&A Games

When reading to children, parents can use Q&A games to stimulate children's desire to read and learn, thus changing the process of parent-child reading into a lively class in which the children can think openly and actively.

Real learning is an exploration of the unknown.

Q&A games are the most important and basic tool in the reading toolbox. Reading is actually a process of exploration, which is a core need for children. Once it is satisfied, children will feel joyful and excited, with a sense of gain and achievement arising spontaneously. They can't feel such pleasure if ready-made answers are given directly, as those in cable cars can't enjoy the fun of climbing a mountain. An interest in reading and learning that arises from the need for exploration is strong and enduring, so it doesn't require external incentives to maintain and strengthen.

According to the research results of some brain scientists, the brain prefers activity to inactivity. Fresh and exciting information can promote brain growth. Exploring the unknown will make the brain secrete more dopamine, which can generate the excitement, energy, and pleasure that we enjoy. If children's desires are satisfied, they will feel happy when reading and learning.

Where does children's direct interest come from? It comes from forming subject consciousness, igniting the desire for knowledge, and gaining unique experience in the process of exploring the unknown world. In the process of reading, parents use their educational wisdom to make the children feel curious and raise relevant questions. It is an approach to opening children's minds and letting them feel the joy of knowledge and have a direct interest in learning.

Therefore, an important purpose of parent-child reading is to use Q&A games to cultivate children's direct interest by posing targeted questions. Children should also be encouraged to have heated discussions and debates with their parents, so as to change the parent-child reading process into a lively class, stimulate their desires for reading and knowledge, and prepare them for more challenges. Solving challenging problems is the best way to develop our brains, because it can form new synaptic connections.

It is known that reading is actually thinking. When reading, a reader needs to think about the meaning of certain words and guess at the development of the plot. Therefore, reading itself is an activity that always requires thinking. When we are reading, our mindsets are continuously switching between "divergent thinking" and "concentrated thinking." Divergent thinking means to work out multiple explanations of complex content based on different standpoints or information. Concentrated thinking is focusing on a certain viewpoint or some information and deeply exploring it. For example, when we think about new ideas or methods as inspired by reading, our thinking is divergent. It helps us expand the scope of thinking. When we need to make a decision, our thinking should be concentrated.

Questioning is an effective tool that allows us to guide our brains to think with the divergent or concentrated model. When we ask a question, our brains are searching for, retrieving, and summarizing information. Effective questioning signifies effective thinking, so parents should not only ask their children questions but also ensure that their children know how to ask questions.

However, there are some misunderstandings about asking questions. We've all met annoying adults who like to ask questions. They don't like to think. They are weak in thinking, working, and acting, and frequently put forward various questions. This is a result of a weak ability to ask questions in childhood. As an adult, do not ask questions easily if the answers can be found just by searching information. The chance to pose questions worth asking should be cherished. Effective interactive training means to raise effective questions and effectively think about them.

✹

Without effective thinking, children will become inactive in thinking as they grow up, easily ask questions, not think hard to identify the authenticity of information, and wait for plausible answers. They will then blindly follow what others have said. How could it be possible for such children to think independently? We all know that reading doesn't fill our brains with knowledge and information at random. It can exercise our capacity for independent and rational thinking through information collection. This is also the real significance of Q&A games.

Let me show you how to play Q&A games with the example of *The Pigeon Needs a Bath*, one of the pigeon books by Mo Willems.

The main character of the pigeon books is a little pigeon. In *Don't Let the Pigeon Drive the Bus*, the little pigeon had already showed his silver tongue. In order to persuade others to let him drive the bus, he made up many excuses and thought about various methods. In *The Pigeon Needs a Bath*, the pigeon was very dirty, but he refused to take a bath anyway and found many plausible reasons to persuade others.

The Pigeon Needs a Bath is a relatively advanced book that contains a lot of philosophical topics, so if we read it with our children, Q&A games can help greatly. "Playing games" and "Q&A" are two sharp tools for cultivating and improving children's thinking and reading skills. Q&A games are one of the best ways to stimulate children's curiosity and continuously enhance their expressing and thinking abilities.

In *Create Super Children Brains*, there are many suggestions for developing all parts of the brain. Among them, parents effectively asking their children questions can help the children understand language, communicate with others, and think about problems. Learning different questioning skills has different impacts on children's language and thinking abilities. Generally speaking, Q&A games can be roughly divided into several types.

First, Q&A games based on narration. What is a Q&A game based on narration? It's easy to understand. Just let children tell you about the main character and the setting. What's there? What happened? For example, the little pigeon in *The Pigeon Needs a Bath* had a "self-confirmation bias." The term sounds obscure, but in easy-to-understand language it means "people always believe what they want to believe." This is exactly what the pigeon did. He always chose to ignore some information in order to prove that he was not dirty. People may often ignore the information that is very evident to others. The information does exist, but they just can't perceive it. It's may be too difficult for children to understand this concept. But we can use narration-based Q&A games to make abstract questions more specific. For example, we can ask: "Which parts of the little pigeon were dirty? Who flew around him?" Specific plots can stimulate children's direct perceptual cognition and help them to better understand the content of a picture book. Storing some fact-based materials in the brain is very helpful for children to observe things carefully and make clear expressions.

Second, Q&A games based on daily scenes. This type is relatively easy to understand. Ask children to think about what happened to them, so that it will be easier for them to think about problems in the place of the main character. For example, the little pigeon was filthy and smelled bad, but he said: "What smell? I didn't smell it." To prove he didn't need a bath, he also insisted that the flies around him were just a coincidence. When having a discussion with children, the parents can introduce a few familiar scenes. For example, "Have you ever pretended not to hear your mom calling you because you don't want to go to sleep? Have you ever avoided looking at your friend because she wants to play with your toys but you don't want her to do so?" Such questions can help children understand the behaviors of the little pigeon.

Third, Q&A games based on reasoning. It means to presume or infer the next or last behavior/status of someone or something: what they are thinking or what will happen, and so on. Children need to analyze, judge, and infer plots based on their knowledge of the main character and relevant aspects of the questions. This kind of thinking training is very helpful for improving their reasoning and empathy abilities. For example, parents can ask, "Why do you think the pigeon can't realize that he smelled bad?" Based on previous examples, children can basically know the answer that because he didn't like taking a bath. "If the pigeon likes to take a bath, can he sniff out his smell?" These hypothetical questions can help children think and infer in a different way and get rid of the "self-confirmation bias." Parents don't need to teach complicated concepts to preschool children, but these children are absolutely able to think about problems based on inference like this. After thinking about their own experience, based on inference and empathy, they can understand that someone choses to ignore something because he/she doesn't like it.

Fourth, Q&A games based on judgment. Judgment means to tell right from wrong. Fact-based judgment is relatively simple, because there are standards to follow. Parents can guide their children to refer to relevant information. However, there are many other things that aren't completely right or wrong. For example, at the beginning of *The Pigeon Needs a Bath*, someone pointed out that the pigeon was dirty and needed to take a bath. But how to define "dirty" or "not dirty"? Is there an absolute standard? The pigeon said, "You know, in some places it is impolite to bathe." So, here is a "relative" concept: bathing is indeed necessary, but it is truly unnecessary to bathe in some places. Parents can thus teach their children about absolute and relative judgment, and discuss the following topics with their children: "How often do we take a bath? If we take a bath once a day and our neighbors take a bath every two days, who is right?" If the children reply, "We are right," the parents can then tell them: "We and our neighbors are both right. There is no absolute standard for the frequency of bathing. It just depends on your own living habits. Many things just have different standards, so there is no absolute right or wrong." These questions may rack the brains of children, but they are very meaningful for giving children multiple perspectives on a problem.

Fifth, Q&A games based on divergent thinking and exploration. These encourage children to get rid of the original frame of a picture book, think and explore into a deeper and wider field, and discuss how they find the answers or why they think in a certain way. Children should give the foundation of their answers, so that they can have a deeper thinking and exploration beyond the surface. For example, the pigeon said, "Life is so short. Why waste it on unimportant things?" When reading this, parents can naturally ask: "Is bathing an unimportant thing? We brush our teeth and wash our hands every day. Is it important?" These questions can make children think about what is important to them. "What are the important things in life? Can we only do important things? Can we ignore those things that are unimportant?" After discussing, parents may find their children think that it is important to graduate from kindergarten and grow up and that it's unimportant to wash hands, brush teeth, or go to sleep, as the pigeon did. If so, parents can tell their children that if you don't finish these unimportant things, you can't achieve big success.

Learning to ask questions and having meaningful discussions with children is the best way to improve their thinking abilities. Thinking is not about pursuing answers. The process of discussion itself is meaningful enough. Thinking training is carried out through such interactions. When children are from three to six years old, Q&A games based on narration are probably the tools most used in graded reading and interactive guidance. However, as children grow up, the parents should also play the other four types of games with their children. Thus, their children can gradually learn how to think indepth about what they are reading. Parents should use proper Q&A games to guide their children to think about about and answer questions (from easy to difficult as the children grow up) from different perspectives, according to the real capability of their children.

Summary

Children's direct interest comes from forming subject consciousness, igniting the desire for knowledge, and gaining unique experience in the process of exploring the unknown world. Therefore, parents can help their children become interested in learning by asking them questions when reading picture books.

When we ask a question, our brains are searching for, retrieving, and summarizing information.

Effective questioning signifies effective thinking, so parents should not only ask their children questions but also ensure that their children know how to ask questions.

When reading with children, the parents can play these five kinds of games: Q&A games based on narration, daily scenes, inference, judgment, and divergent thinking and exploration, separately or collectively based on children's interest.

Expert guidance: What roles should parents play in parent-child reading?

Expert Guidance

For children older than four years, the parents should act as a reading-aloud expert or teacher when reading a picture book. Parents should enlighten their children about reading in a professional fashion and help them observe the world from more perspectives.

Many parents are used to interacting with their children in a childish tone when reading picture books. For early reading, this manner of speaking can make parents look more amiable. However, speaking to older children with this tone can't enhance their cognition. Therefore, parents need to guide the children older than four years by different means to perform grade reading. During parent-child reading, sometimes the parents need to play the role of a read-aloud expert or teacher and act in a professional way to enlighten their children about reading.

Why should parents act as experts? Yohji Yamamoto, a famous Japanese designer, said: "'Self' is invisible, bumping into something else, and rebounding to understand itself. So, you can know about yourself after bumping into something strong, formidable, and of high quality." This passage explains why parents should play the professional roles of experts, strong men or women, or teachers to guide their children of this age. Children can find out who they are by referring to unfamiliar identities and roles, especially through the appeal of professionalism.

The growth and development of humans are, to a large extent, like a bat flying and exploring in darkness. Everyone can send their own ultrasonic wave, which rebounds after it bumps into different objects. We learn in this way to recognize directions, catch prey, and find ourselves. Therefore, playing the role of a professional reciter, expert, or teacher can help children observe the world from more perspectives and encourage them to explore and perceive the diversity and richness of the world. If children can't have the feelings of staying in different scenes, it will be difficult for them to understand what is good, bad, fake, professional, noble, or base.

Expert guidance, similar to playing the roles of strangers, can create a sense of distance and involve children in certain sense of ceremony. During daily normal parent-child reading, the children will fall into a normal state of enjoying listening to stories. Once the role of the storyteller is changed, the children will experience various changes and possibilities that they will also encounter in life.

Although adults have seemingly become used to our habitual selves, our performance may be surprisingly excellent in a sudden strange situation. When we get along with a new person with a different background, our abilities of expression and communication will also improve accordingly. We may later recall that experience. This is the power of chance when meeting a stranger.

Scientists have also confirmed the existence of this power. The research team of Walter Mischel, a famous American psychologist, monitored the brain activities of some college students with a magnetic resonance imager. At the beginning of the experiment, the subjects were asked to think about their current selves, and the MRI instrument showed that the middle parts of their brain cortices began to change. This unique pattern of activity is called the "self mode." Then, when they were imagining a strange professor as requested by the researchers, the instrument showed that another pattern of activity in the same area of their brain cortices was activated. It was called the "stranger model."

In the end, they were asked to "think about what they would look like ten years later." It turned out that when thinking about their future, everyone had different feelings and brain activities. But the brain activities of most subjects were more like the "stranger model." In other words, everyone looked at their future self as if looking at a stranger. It follows that strangers, unfamiliar characters and scenes, are more closely related to everyone's future. The freshness and stimulus brought by strangeness make it easier for people to feel the magical power of longing. The jobs that most of us do nowadays actually have a lot to do with the unfamiliar scenes, persons, or status we experienced or met or experienced in childhood. This is also the psychological basis for parents to use the method of expert guidance in the parent-child reading process of graded reading.

Let me show you how to help children master necessary new words and improve the fluency of reading with the method of expert guidance by taking *The Polar Express* as an example.

First, parents set their roles as an expert or a teacher, arrive at the proper tones and gestures, and read aloud with their children as professionally as they can. While reading aloud, parents should guide their children to look at the pictures carefully and memorize the new words in the text. If children run into unfamiliar content, the parents are supposed to explain them as an expert does.

For example, before telling the story of *The Polar Express*, parents may talk with their children about the background of Christmas. *The Polar Express* is a picture book that teaches children to cherish childlike innocence. When introducing Christmas, parents should start from the specific and interesting aspects. Don't make it as boring as popular science.

Share fun, colorful, and exciting details about related subject matter, so children will understand that they can gain so much knowledge through reading. Thus, they will be more interested in it.

When reading *The Polar Express*, parents can guide their children to notice details in the pictures and link the knowledge gained from the picture book with children's previous experience. Parents may ask: "Look at this train, does it have any differences with those we have taken? Yes! It has a chimney, just like the Thomas train. Right! This is a steam train. Do you remember what fuels a steam train?" Connecting new and old knowledge like this is one of the best ways to learn.

We can also use the internet to conveniently explain what is difficult to express simply by words. For example, we can ask our children, "Where is the North Pole? Does anyone live there? What is their lifestyle?" We can then search for and look at photos and videos of Longyearbyen in Norway. We can tell them this city is only 1,300 kilometers away from the North Pole, and that it is the northernmost city on earth. The story of *The Polar Express* may happen here.

When finishing the last sentence, "the bell still rings for me as it does for all who truly believe," parents can ask, "Do you believe this silver bell will ring?" When discussing whether Santa really exists, children will have many questions, making it a good chance for effective education. We should tell children that believing these beautiful things will make your life full of hope.

In front of children, parents are not only storytellers but also experts who know everything. If parents make some preparation, their children will have a yearning for reading. Why not do it?

Summary

During the daily parent-child reading, the children enjoy listening to stories. If the storyteller becomes an "expert," children will look forward to infinite possibilities, just as adults improve their abilities of expressing and communicating when interacting with experts. When using the method of expert guidance to read a picture book with children, the parents should first set their roles as an expert or a teacher, determine the proper tones and gestures, and read aloud as professionally as possible, thus guiding the children to think.

Behavior adjustment:
How to apply book learning in real life

Behavior Adjustment

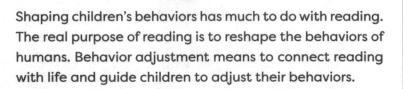

Shaping children's behaviors has much to do with reading. The real purpose of reading is to reshape the behaviors of humans. Behavior adjustment means to connect reading with life and guide children to adjust their behaviors.

On the surface, reading can improve our cognition and thinking abilities. But its real purpose is to reshape our behaviors. In particular, shaping children's behaviors has a lot to do with reading. As a reading tool, behavior adjustment means to link reading with children's lives and guide them to adjust their behaviors. It is also a very basic method of early reading enlightenment.

Almost every picture book is a certain reflection on children's life. For children aged from three to six, reading picture books can enhance their abilities to read and understand pictures and texts, and it can also give them many chances to choose their own behaviors. Picture books can be used as the standards and references for children to shape their behaviors.

Reading and learning are essentially brain remodeling. Behaviors are closely related to the brain. People's behaviors are controlled by their brains. The brain is truly useful only if it can cause behaviors.

The nervous systems of humans can be divided into the central nervous system and the peripheral nervous system. The former includes the brain and spinal cord, and the rest of the nerve branches belong to the latter system. Brain scientists generally believe that the brain needs to receive neural signals from the peripheral nervous system in order to respond and needs to transmit signals in order to cause behaviors. If the brain is independent of the body and can't sense or receive any information, it will lose its function as the nerve center. Only when the brain is connected with the outside world and can cause corresponding behaviors can it be regarded as the real "brain." Early reading enlightenment means to use the visual and auditory organs to obtain information, repeatedly stimulate and shape the brain, and thus shape children's behaviors.

⁂

Children's ability to adjust their own behaviors is affected by genetic and environmental factors. The home has significant influences on the behavior self-adjustment of children, especially in the process of reading, which contains much information. The impacts of reading on children's behaviors are mainly about helping them effectively control impulsive responses.

Children's self-control abilities develop quickly at the age of from three to six. Therefore, one of the important functions of family reading enlightenment is to effectively promote children's ability to adjust their behavior by reading. Parent-child reading can support the parent-child relationship and encourage children to behave themselves. The research on children's behaviors shows that rule-governed behaviors are closely related to the development of children's self-control. In high-quality reading enlightenment, parents should encourage the children to learn the rules of conduct contained in picture books and teach them to effectively control and be responsible for their behaviors. This is one of the key points of reading enlightenment for children of this age. These rules are actually a kind of social standard about collaboration and harmonious coexistence. Reading can socialize these standards through extensive individual behaviors.

Therefore, from the ages of three to six and through parent-child reading, children can fully understand and accept the rules and requirements in books for the situations similar to real-life scenarios. They can check the justification of individual behaviors and purposes by referring to these basic social rules, and thus achieve cognitive and behavioral balance. They can control and adjust their behaviors according to relevant rules. This is the real significance of "behavior adjustment" in early reading enlightenment. To give a simple example, when reading *The Elephant and the Bad Baby* with parents, the children may notice that the bad boy took the things that belonged to others without saying "Thank you," so he was chased by many people and couldn't return to his home. When children face similar situations in the future, they will reflect on themselves and then take the initiative to express their gratitude to others. They will act in accordance with social rules.

When teaching children about rules of conduct through reading, the parents shouldn't forcefully set life rules and standards or enforce certain norms. The key is to let children autonomously choose a proper way of acting under the unconscious influence of their parents. Developing self-control in this way actually doesn't need external supervision. It is similar to the self-reflection ability emphasized in Chinese culture; in other words, the readers can manage and control their behaviors flexibly and adaptively according to what they have read.

From ages three to six, children's physical and psychological conditions develop under fixed laws; reading itself also has various characteristics. Family reading should be carried out based on the knowledge of these laws. Fang Suzhen, an expert in reading picture books, once published a report on the reading abilities and behaviors of children up to the age of twelve and made a list about the features of each stage. Then, what are the features of children's reading abilities and behaviors from three to six?

Table 2: Reading and Behavioral Features of Children Ages Three to Six Years Old

Three Years Old	
Behavioral Features	• Understand the appearance of objects. • Like bright colors. • Have different kinds of fun in the imaginary and real world. • Can turn pages and remember some sentences in a story or retell the story outline. • Can recite an entire sentence or story and don't allow others to change the plots they have said. • Can tell familiar stories to themselves.
Suitable Books	• Imaginative, exaggerated, funny books. • Books with simple plots and those about morality and emotions. • Books about rhymes and counting numbers and pop-up books. • Books on family affection and friendship. • Popular science books related to living habits, animals, and food.

(Continued)

Behavioral Guidance for Parents	• Read stories at a fixed time. • Connect book content with life experience at any time and anywhere. • Be patient when children tirelessly ask to read the same book or tell the same story.
Four Years Old	
Behavioral Features	• Can turn pages one by one and distinguish subtle differences in books. • Can listen to long stories. • Enjoy reading and playing independently; like repeating familiar stories. • Like role play and listening to stories; can recognize their own names and familiar words.
Suitable Books	• Longer stories with more complex plots. • Picture books with more detailed pictures. • Picture books without words to practice imagination. • Books related to living environment, school, friends, and animals. • Books that teach maps, shapes, sizes, and colors.
Behavioral Guidance for Parents	• Encouarge children to tell stories. • Ask children to guess book titles according to the pictures and the words they can recognize. • Encourage children to draw pictures and learn to read. • Take children to a library and borrow some books, or go to a bookstore to read a book.

Five Years Old	
Behavioral Features	• Can clearly understand the meaning of words and ask their parents to read with them. • Understand that text is meaningful and can express complex emotions. • Know story structures and can retell stories. • Distinguish things based on subjective judgment of right and wrong. • Can read aloud to others and recognize familiar new words.
Suitable Books	• Folktales with distinct standards of good and bad. • Books about daily life and how to solve problems. • Fairy tales with imaginative plots. • Topics about physical development and autonomy. • Books fit for children's psychology, and those about interpersonal relationships, and expression of love.
Behavioral Guidance for Parents	• Tell bedtime stories. • Encourage children to tell stories to parents. • Encourage children to think about problems in books; ask them to predict or adapt the ending; stimulate their imagination.
Six Years Old	
Behavioral Features	• Like exploration and can guess the trend of plots. • Can perform familiar stories and express how much they like or dislike a story. • Can understand time and numbers; show great enthusiasm for discovering the world and how it works. • Can observe pictures quietly and listen to longer stories. • Can tell important plots and express their opinions in group discussions.

(Continued)

Suitable Books	• Picture books on science knowledge. • Stories about families and communities. • Picture books about value judgment, interpersonal relationships, or differences in gender roles. • Picture books with more complex plots and more detailed drawings. • Books on astronomy and geography. • Classic fairy tales. • Books about emotional skills. • Don't force children to recite or write.
Behavioral Guidance for Parents	• Encourage children to express ideas by speaking, drawing, or other means. • Read stories aloud with children and enjoy the content and rhythms. • Continue stories with children.

From the above list of the behaviors of children between the ages of three to six and the guidance for their parents, we can see that proper guidance by parents absolutely can help children to improve their perceptual, cognitive, and behavioral abilities at appropriate ages. Although the characteristics and progress are different for each child, the list above can still be used as an important reference for parent-child reading.

Parents should consciously optimize and reshape their children's cognition, brains, and behaviors through reading. They should use reading to set up some guiding thoughts and form decisive and firm norms on some key issues. Don't threaten children or give them mandatory directives. Instead, let them realize that certain norms can't be challenged casually. Parents also need to provide some clear cognitive directions. Don't be ambiguous or narrow minded. Give children the proper rights to make independent choices and let them experience the consequences of violations within a controllable scope. We must let children take consequences and then work with them to find solutions, rather than simply blaming and complaining. This is the essence of behavior adjustment.

Summary

Reading and learning are essentially brain remodeling. Picture books can be used as the standards and references for children to shape their behaviors. With the method of behavior adjustment, children can manage and control their behaviors flexibly and adaptively according to the rules of conduct implied in picture books and under the imperceptible influence of their parents.

Parents can carry out parent-child reading according to the reading abilities and behavioral features of children aged from three to six and guide them properly to improve their perceptual, cognitive, and behavioral abilities.

Chapter 6
Training Children's Comprehensive Reading Ability

Milestone method: When to pick harder books for children

Milestone Method

To use the milestone method in reading enlightenment, parents should record the important milestones in children's reading. For example, they finish reading a fifty-page picture book or retell a story for the first time. All these achievements can be recorded in a milestone list to encourage children to move on.

Many people think "milestones" should be very good things that happened in life. For example, a student performed much better than usual in the college entrance exam and was admitted to a key university; an employee was promoted to leadership; a start-up company went public quickly. Should only major events be called milestones? In fact, the milestone method used in reading enlightenment is not so complicated or serious. Milestones include not only very important things. They are key turns, whether good or bad, that can affect children's reading and learning behaviors. Even a key mistake, such as not being able to understand something after reading it twice, can be called a milestone.

For children between the ages of three and six years old, any little progress in reading is an important milestone. For example, a child can read a long sentence after their parents, tell a simple complete story to their parents, or understand an idiom for the first time. These things may be unimportant to adults, but they are important milestones in reading enlightenment of children.

It is very easy to use the milestone method, just taking important turns in children's reading as milestones to encourage them to continue. For example, divide children's bookshelves into two areas: books unread and books finished. If children finish reading a picture book, that book should be moved from the unread area to the finished area. It can give children a sense of accomplishment, which encourages them to reach further goals and read more books. If a child finishes reading a fifty-page picture book for the first time, parents can write it down in the milestone list to motivate them.

The milestone method is very useful, but it has been ignored by many parents. One possible reason is that many families didn't have enough books before the children were born, and parents themselves lack a good reading habit. Therefore, it's hard for them to read many books with their children and encourage their children to read. A more important reason is that parents are not experts in reading enlightenment. They lack a clear and accurate understanding of the milestone method. Some may even have misunderstandings about it. So, they don't know how to encourage their children with this method. In fact, when children needed reading, many parents began to buy many books, which were just put on shelves, because parents can't read through them with their children. As time goes by, the books were no longer suitable for children to read, and thus remained on shelves. As long as parents divide these books into two categories and set up different reading collections, the milestone method can be used to arouse children's sense of accomplishment, encourage them, and guide them to read more books.

How to Properly Use This Method

First, set milestones according to the characteristics of children's cognitive development. In order to determine what behaviors can be regarded as important milestones, we need to understand the cognitive characteristics of children aged from three to five.

Table 3 shows children's cognitive characteristics as summarized by the National Association for the Education of Young Children. After clearly understanding the characteristics of each stage of children's cognitive development, parents can arrange proper reading activities for each stage based on these features. Thus, the milestone method can give children positive feedback and timely encouragement. Only this kind of reading enlightenment is truly scientific. Of course, every child is unique. So, when exploiting children's potential, the parents must consider their features.

Table 3: Cognitive Characteristics of Children Ages Three to Five Years Old

Three Years Old	Understand what is the past and present. Can role-play with dolls or stuffed toys. Can sort things by their features (shapes, sizes, colors, etc.). Can concentrate for five to fifteen minutes. Begin to ask why.
Four Years Old	Can picture a specific person with at least two body parts. Know and can tell where they live. Can count to five and understand the concept of counting. Can describe pictures; especially can tell stories based on their own drawings. Can count to at least ten. Basically understand the concepts of time and dates.
Five Years Old	Can picture a specific person with at least four body parts. Can draw basic geometric figures by imitation. Can try to write numbers.

Second, let children clearly perceive their progress and know its great significance. Many reading goals we set for our children are not specific enough. For example, "You have to read carefully; you should finish this book." Without the milestone method, children will easily give up when meeting obstacles, and turn to the TV, smartphones, or games. If we can use interesting milestones to encourage them to read, the whole process of enlightenment will be much smoother.

For example, we can draw some milestone cards to record their important milestone events. We can also establish a medal system for parent-child reading. Children can be rewarded with a medal for each book they finish or each milestone they reach as encouragement. When making medals, parents can refer to the objects that their children like, such as cartoon characters including Peppa Pig or Disney or Marvel figures. Parents can prepare a box for their children to collect reading medals, or put a medal board on the bookshelf.

We can also make special medals according to the countries from which the authors come. For example, use the British flag and French flag to represent the authors from the UK and France, respectively. When children have read a certain number of books from the UK or France, they can receive an "England medal" or a "France medal." With these medals, children can not only learn to recognize flags but also feel a sense of ceremony because certain milestones have been reached.

These medal awards can change children's reading achievements, acquired under the professional guidance of their parents, into moments with extraordinary significance that can motivate them to overcome more challenges. Therefore, milestones can not only highlight children's achievements in each stage but also demonstrate their growth process. This is the significance of milestones. To realize desired effects, milestones should be clearly defined honors that can be perceived by children and are very meaningful. This is the motivational effect of setting proper milestones on reading and learning.

Third, further visualize children's reading skills. Parents can record videos of key milestones. Their children can then feel their progress by comparing their performance in these videos. Each milestone can be recorded in an unforgettable and precious video. What will happen if children can compare, by watching these videos, the number of books they have read and their reading abilities at the age of two and at the age of three and a half? They will immediately feel their significant changes: "Look, at that time I could only listen to my mom reading picture books, but now I can read by myself." How wonderful this moment is for children! However, few parents record such milestones.

Most children don't like reading because they were not encouraged by milestones in the stage of reading enlightenment. Their parents may have said, "Wow, how big of you!" But they didn't record those important moments and failed to review and share them with their children. They have neglected these very important things. Most parents have put a lot of effort into parent-child reading, but their results vary greatly due to a little negligence.

The "Peak-End Rule" is a behavioral law frequently emphasized in *Decisive*, written by Chip Heath and Dan Heath, famous professors of organizational behaviors. "Peak-End" means the most impressive moment of a certain experience (i.e., the instant when we feel the strongest emotions, whether good or bad) and the end of that experience. We easily forget the other moments of that experience. It means we tend to be impressed with important moments. The key of our memory lies in the peak feelings we have when reaching these important milestones. Parents should take advantages of major moments of glory related to reading and learning and set more important milestones. Thus, children can take the initiative to read what is boring or difficult but important. This is the guidance for using the milestone method in parent-child reading.

Summary

Parents can accurately set important reading milestones by referring to the cognitive characteristics of children ages three to six. Medals, points, or other rewards can be used as timely encouragement to let children clearly perceive their progress and know its great significance. Parents can also record videos of key reading milestones the children have reached, from which they can feel their progress by comparison. At this moment, they may have peak feelings.

Collation of clues: What to do if children fear reading books with complex plots

Collation of Clues

For everyone, reading a book is like walking in a maze. There are seemingly countless paths, but only one leads to the exit. By collating clues, children can sort out useful information to explore in the maze of a picture book and find a way out.

Before introducing how to collate clues, I will tell you a Greek myth about Theseus's victory over the minotaur. Theseus was a king of Athens. He was once ordered to kill the minotaur on Crete. It wasn't a difficult task for the wise and heroic Theseus, but the biggest trouble was how to walk out of the monster's maze. Before setting out, he met Ariadne, a smart princess who gave him a thread and a sharp sword. Before entering the maze, Theseus tied one end of the thread to the pillar at the door. With the sword in hand, he unraveled the thread as he went deeper. In the end, he managed to kill the minotaur and found the way out by following the thread.

Sometimes the process of reading is similar to this story. Gaining knowledge and developing cognition are like killing the minotaur, but if we don't have any clues, like the thread in the story, we will be easily lost in a maze of enormous knowledge and content. When reading, we also need some really effective clues, which have the same function as Ariadne's thread. These clues can help us not get lost in the maze of the world and knowledge. Someone thinks, "there are a thousand Hamlets in a thousand people's eyes." In other words, every book is a unique maze for every reader. There are many roads, but most of them lead to a dead end. If we don't have Ariadne's thread, we will get trapped in the cognitive maze of a book forever.

This is the importance of clue collation in early reading enlightenment. Reading, on the surface, is a process of acquiring information, but what is really important is not the information itself, but the information about the information; in other words, the clues, or we call it the navigation system of cognition. Now that clues are so important, how can children learn to find truly useful clues in the process of reading and cognition?

"Searching" and "collating" are two core methods.

The reading materials for children have many clues but children generally don't know how to search for and collate them. We adults also lack these abilities. We have never been seriously trained to search and collate information, so we can never meet our demands with existing resources. There are various unbreakable limits on the way to achieving our goals. We seem to be caught in a cognition maze. Cognitive progress is actually achieved in the process of finding useful clues among enormous specious possibilities. In other words, cognition generally means to find useful clues.

Then, what is the collation of clues? In fact, reading and acquiring useful information is like a division formula, in which possibility is the denominator and the clue is the numerator. As there could be only one effective clue, more possibilities will result in smaller ratios. So, collating clues means to delete fake possibilities so as to lower the value of the denominator. When the numerator is infinitely close to the denominator, we can discover the real relationship between cognition and truth.

※

Theories are abstract, so let me show you how to search for and collate clues by taking a picture book as an example.

For narrative picture books, there are several types of clues in general: object clues, person clues, event clues, emotion clues, time clues, and the clues about what one has seen and heard.

The first type refers to the clues about specific things or their characteristics. For example, the clue of *The Biggest Cake in the World* is the biggest cake in the world, which is always mentioned in the story.

The second type refers to the clues about persons or their characteristics. For example, the entire surprising story of *The Three Robbers* develops around the three robbers.

The third type refers to the clues about major events. For example, *Angry Arthur* is about the moment when Arthur's mom didn't allow Arthur to watch TV, so he became angry.

The fourth type are clues about thoughts and emotions. For example, in the *Last Stop on Market Street*, the attitude of Jie, the main character, changed from complaining to embracing the beauty of the ordinary world. This process of emotional transformation was linked up by Jie's feelings about every passenger on the bus and about the world.

The fifth type is time clues. Stories develop in a clear chronological order. For example, *The Rainbow Flower* tells a story of a flower who uses her petals to help others and share the joy of life in each season. The story goes on as seasons are changing: (Spring) Winter passed away and spring came. The sun came out and . . . (Summer) These days, the sunshine was very strong. (Autumn) The daytime became shorter and shorter. It was autumn already. (Winter) Very soon, everything was covered with snow, leaving a vast expanse of whiteness.

The sixth type is the clues about what the main character has seen and heard. For example, *The Lightning Fish Named Nick* is based on what the little yellow croaker has seen and heard on the journey of seeking his dream. He wanted to be a fruit fish, rooster fish, onion fish, rainbow fish, or cloud fish. In the end, he realized that reading made him want to be himself. Reading aims not to make children become others, but to discover and realize themselves.

After knowing the above six types of clues that arise when reading picture books, we can consciously seek these clues when reading a picture book to our children. Then, we should find out the clues that are truly logical through collation and comparison, so as to help our children better understand the content of the book and improve their reading abilities and comprehension.

What are specific ways to help children search for and sort out clues?

Take time clues as an example. When reading a picture book with children, the parents may mark the words about time with a highlighter, such as the changes of seasons, the ages of characters, and the years passed by. Based on this information, children can organize the time clues in the book. For example, when reading *Four Thirty*, a classic Korean picture book, parents can remind their children to notice that it was half past four when the little girl asked her grandpa what time it was. She played for a long time. The sky was dark and lights were on when she returned home. So, parents can ask children to notice these details, which showed it was definitely not four thirty anymore. Sorting out time clues in this way can make content clearer, and children can realize time is passing while the little girl was playing.

When reading an early chapter book with relatively complex story lines, parents can write down time nodes beside relevant words, and then put them in a normal or reverse order. They can also put forward some questions and ask their children to find correct time nodes and infer main plots based on time clues. The training on searching and collating clues can help children strengthen their memory and improve their learning abilities and insight.

In addition to directly seeking the above six types of clues, parents can also retrieve and sort clues by extracting keywords. Every picture book has a theme, which is made up of some keywords. So, parents can find clues from book titles and the words or objects that appear frequently. Parents can guide their children to read through a book, and then look for keywords related to its theme. At first, children may find many "keywords" that are actually not important, so parents must discuss them with their children, remove unimportant ones, and only keep the keywords that are really relevant to the theme. By doing so, we may find three or four keywords that can summarize the real theme and content of a picture book. For example, when reading *Duck on a Bike*, we may find the "duck," "cow," "sheep" and other animals, and the actions like "riding," "pedaling," "ringing a bell," "standing on the seat with one foot," etc. We can notice that the riding skills of the duck improved a lot, and the attitudes of other animals also changed from admiring to unwilling and finally to happy. When retrieving and collating clues, children can also abstract content and think deeply. This training on searching for keyword clues also helps to improve children's rational thinking and develop their cognitive abilities.

Clues are the foundation for learning, independent thinking, and insight. When children are from three to six years old, parents must demonstrate how to find, sort, and analyze clues and draw sound conclusions based on these clues. They should also encourage and guide their children to do these activities in daily life. Such reading enlightenment can not only make children enjoy reading but also improve their reading abilities.

Summary

Reading, on the surface, is a process of acquiring information, but what really matters is the information about the information: the clues. Parents should ensure their children have learned the two core methods, namely, "searching" and "collating." For picture books with story lines, there are several types of clues in general: object clues, person clues, event clues, emotion clues, time clues, and the clues about what one has seen and heard. Every picture book has a theme, which is made up of some keywords. Therefore, parents can guide their children to find clues based on the keywords that frequently appear.

Plot map: How to teach children to read heavy books

Plot Map

Help children to draw a plot map of a book based on the mind mapping or time line, in order to help them understand complex plots. Children can also develop their brains and improve their reading abilities when drawing the plot map.

We all know that the brain can be divided into the left brain and right brain. The left part is mainly responsible for abstract thinking, such as logic, language, analysis, judgment, and writing. Its way of thinking is continuous and analytical. Therefore, it is widely called the "abstract brain," "academic brain," or "language brain." The right brain is mainly responsible for figurative work, such as image, memory, intuition, emotion, vision, arts, and imagination. Therefore, many people refer to it as the "image brain," "art brain," and "memory brain." Many parents pay much attention to the effective development of both left and right brains. "Whole-brain education" is also popular around the world. It is an efficient learning method that can inspire and train the left and right brains together. Then, how to use the method of whole-brain education in the reading of picture books? Plot maps can help a lot.

The plot map has two keywords: "plot" and "map." It means to draw a plot map of a book based on mind mapping or the time line, making it easier for children to understand complicated plots.

In this process, parents should also guide children to coordinate and develop their left and right brains and improve their reading abilities. Mind mapping takes advantage of the left brain's functions about words, logic, and induction and the functions of the right brain about colors, pictures, and imagination. Therefore, when children are drawing plot maps, their left and right brains must be coordinating with each other.

When reading a picture book with a relatively complicated plot to children, we can use the plot map to help them improve their reading abilities and learning efficiency. If they can easily understand complicated content, they won't be afraid of reading. Children will change from "I am forced to read" to "I want to read," and they will have greater initiative and enthusiasm in reading. High efficiency of reading and learning can save lots of time, so children can have more time to play. Children wish to play happily, read gladly, and learn efficiently. Parents also want their children to do so.

Tony Buzan, the inventor of mind mapping, repeatedly emphasized that everyone has an equal chance to become wise, regardless of their family or educational background. Tony once told a story about a little boy answering his teacher's questions. There was a little boy whose grades were not good. The teachers all thought he was mediocre and had no great future. The boy himself also gradually admitted this "fact." Once a teacher asked him to write down the uses of paper clips. He replied, after thinking, "Sorry, I'm too stupid." But the teacher insisted on guiding him to think divergently with the mind mapping. Finally, the boy wrote dozens of uses. At that moment, pleasure and excitement arose in his dull eyes, and his whole body was enveloped by the light of confidence and wisdom. The teacher was amazed and kept praising him as a genius. Mind mapping can coordinate the left and right brains. It can combine abstract logic with divergent imagination. This is the brain-science principle of this method.

The plot map should be used when children have accumulated a certain amount of reading experience. When children begin to read picture books with more words, over fifty pages, and with more complex plots, they will meet obstacles in reading. If without proper methods and guidance, they will shrink back from difficulties. We have gradually made children become interested in reading, so we must timely provide supportive reading methods to encourage them. B. F. Skinner, an American psychologist, proposed the theory of positive and negative reinforcement. The theory believes that, in order to achieve their purposes, humans or animals will act on themselves and the environment. If the consequences are beneficial to themselves, they will take these actions repeatedly, and this is called positive reinforcement. If the consequences are harmful, these actions will be reduced or disappear, and this is called negative reinforcement. Some children lose interest in reading or learning because they are frustrated by the difficulties that arise. If they seldom feel a sense of accomplishment in reading and learning and are often neglected or criticized by their parents or teachers, they will give up and turn to negative reinforcement. At that time, it is too late to remedy.

To improve children's comprehension and reading abilities, *The Biggest Cake in the World* is used to illustrate how to draw plot maps with the mind mapping.

The first is the Circle Map, mainly used to define a concept. It consists of two circles. The inner circle uses words, numbers, or pictures to determine the theme, and the outer circle uses pictures or words to describe the theme. In *The Biggest Cake in the World*, Leonardo da Vinci, on a whim, planned to build a wedding hall for a duke with the world's largest cake. Parents can work with their children to list the ingredients needed to make the cake in a circle mind map.

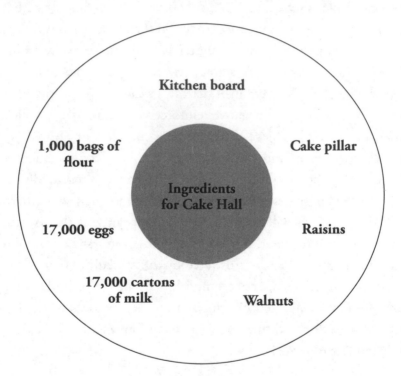

The second is the bubble map, which is used to describe the characteristics of things. The circle map is used to define concepts, but the bubble map is to describe themes in the central bubbles with descriptive words. This is the essential difference between them. For example, there is a page in *The Biggest Cake in the World* that is particularly suitable for drawing a bubble map: the page describing the personalities of Duke Sforza.

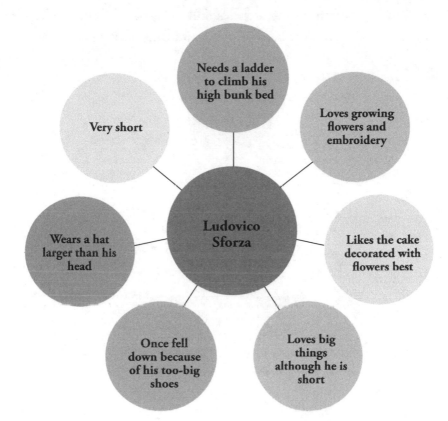

The third is the double bubble map. The double bubble map is made up of two bubble maps. It can compare the similarities and differences of two things, enhancing children's ability to think, compare, and analyze. In reading training, it can be used to compare features of the characters and environments. Of course, we can also use it to compare similarities and differences between two stories. When reading *The Biggest Cake in the World*, we can draw a double bubble map to compare the personalities of Duke Sforza and Princess Durst, and then see how their acts were different because of different personalities. The duke was very angry because the cake was eaten by the animals and villagers, but the duchess told him that it was the best kindness and thus pacified the duke.

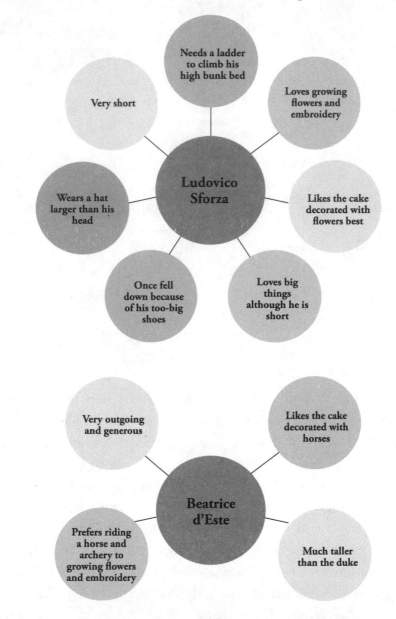

The fourth is the tree map. It looks like a tree and is used for classification. The trunk represents a theme, and the branches mean different categories. The first-level branch can be further divided to create new subcategories. Based on the book, we can draw a tree map about the tools needed by da Vinci to make the cake.

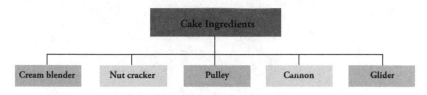

The fifth is the flow map. A flow map, as its name indicates, describes the sequence of events and their internal logical relationships. The main character in the book is the famous painter da Vinci. Of course, we know he is also an inventor, military strategist, architect, and excellent cook. Da Vinci accepted the task of planning a wedding ceremony for a duke. The whole story develops based on how da Vinci completes this task. We can guide children to write down da Vinci's steps to the accomplishment. This flow map can clearly show the flow of da Vinci's logic.

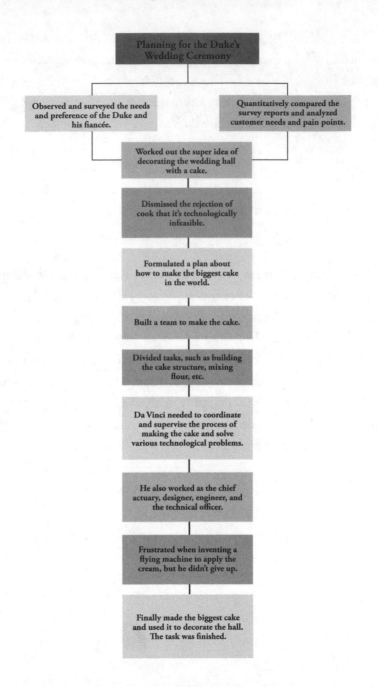

Planning for the Duke's Wedding Ceremony

Observed and surveyed the needs and preference of the Duke and his fiancée.

Quantitatively compared the survey reports and analyzed customer needs and pain points.

Worked out the super idea of decorating the wedding hall with a cake.

Dismissed the rejection of cook that it's technologically infeasible.

Formulated a plan about how to make the biggest cake in the world.

Built a team to make the cake.

Divided tasks, such as building the cake structure, mixing flour, etc.

Da Vinci needed to coordinate and supervise the process of making the cake and solve various technological problems.

He also worked as the chief actuary, designer, engineer, and the technical officer.

Frustrated when inventing a flying machine to apply the cream, but he didn't give up.

Finally made the biggest cake and used it to decorate the hall. The task was finished.

Summary

When reading a picture book with a relatively complicated plot to children, parents can use the plot map to help them improve the children's reading abilities and learning efficiency.

Mind mapping can combine abstract logic with divergent imagination and coordinate the left and right brains, thus comprehensively developing children's brains.

The types of mind maps used frequently include: circle map, bubble map, double bubble map, tree map, and flow map.

Imagination and verification: How to mobilize children's initiative for reading

Imagination and Verification

Parents encourage the children to imagine and make reasonable guesses in the process of parent-child reading and verify or question previous plots in terms of what they read later.

This is the method of imagination and verification.

The method of imagination and verification uses logical inference to determine whether the material that is being read is reasonable and scientific. In parent-child reading, children should learn to question what they have read before in terms of the content they read later. For example, when reading a page, parents can stop and say, "Wait, isn't it contradictory to previous plots?" Then, they can find the conflicts together with their children and check if these conflicts are caused by the children's misunderstanding of previous or present content.

Some parents are easily confused about the method of imagination and verification and the method of inference we have mentioned before. Actually, it's easy to differentiate them: the latter focuses on inspiring children to think and read, while the former places a higher value on understanding and verifying the material being read. It is a process of connecting reading content and automatically verifying it. Self-assessment and self-adjustment based on the understanding of reading content play an important role in cultivating reading-oriented minds and developing brains.

Brain scientists and neuroscientists have verified on many occasions that those good at continuously absorbing new information and stimuli during reading are adept at thinking and analyzing. They have more synaptic junctions and more complex connections among brain nerves than other people. During the process of self-examination and self-adjustment, one needs to analyze, judge, select, monitor, evaluate, and regulate. All these activities are basically about processing new information. They can stimulate brain neurons to keep discharging and producing more dendrites, making the brain more agile and efficient.

The process of imagination and verification is a basic method of graded reading. Why? This method aims to establish a memory model of correct responses, reinforce it, and amend the neural networks to note incomplete or incorrect information. The process of imagination and verification is an important mechanism of information feedback, which can continuously carry out deterministic tests to reduce the uncertainty of judgment. Children need to participate in the reading process by making right or wrong predictions. Frequent formative evaluation and corrective feedback are the key methods to promote long-term memory, develop reasoning abilities, and analyze executive functions.

It is through self-adjustment that the brain consciously corrects misinformation found in the neural network so that it can accurately reflect and process external information and further enhance brain sensitivity to correct responses. Self-adjustment allows children to have a better reading or learning experience with the fluctuations of dopamine levels and ensure they begin to love reading or improve their learning efficiency in a good mood. What's more, self-adjustment can also promote the metabolism of neurons, trim some neurons, strengthen others, and produce new neurons, and thus develop the brain.

The tool of imagination and verification aims to develop children's abilities to think and reflect. It is strongly emphasized throughout the process of reading enlightenment, in order to help children form the habit of reflecting. It is a science-based tool that can improve the effects of family reading enlightenment and truly enhance children's reading, learning, and cognition abilities.

✦

Here the picture book *Belinda The Ballerina* is used to explain how to imagine and verify.

Open the first page and ask children to find what makes Belinda different from other ballerinas. Does she have longer legs? Does she dance more beautifully? Does her dress look better? Or is it because her feet are different? Ask children to use their imagination and guess what makes Belinda special. They can guess that her feet are too big. Then, ask them what difficulties she may have when dancing ballet? What special experience will she undergo? Will she look awkward, fall down, or not be graceful? Children will have their own judgment and imagination. However, the following plot is likely to be different from what they imagine, which will be verified later.

When moving to the second and third pages, children will find Belinda's dance is very agile and beautiful, but her big feet have become the biggest trouble. Why? Because she felt inferior for her big feet? Or was there any accident that affected her performance? These questions will guide them to imagine what will happen later, and parents shouldn't give answers too early.

When reading the next page, children can notice that Belinda doesn't think there is anything wrong with her feet. However, just as she went on the stage to compete in the contest, the judges immediately yelled at her to stop. Why? Why did the judges look terrified and frustrated? Now let children continue to use their imagination and guess what happened. They may have various guesses. Any guess is okay.

Next, read what the judges said and accordingly verify children's conjectures. We have watched many talent shows or competitions on TV with our children, and the judges usually encourage the players politely. However, the judges in the story are very unkind. Then, let children guess what Belinda will do. Or, ask them, "What will you do if you are criticized or laughed at in a competition by the judges? Will you continue to work hard, or simply give up your dreams so as not to be looked down on?" Children may have their own judgment. They may say, "I'll give up" or "I can learn something else with my advantages."

In the story, Belinda lost her confidence after being humiliated and sadly gave up her dream of dancing. However, she didn't give up herself completely. She still worked hard to be useful to society. She found a job in a restaurant as a waitress, trying hard to live a meaningful life. When reading these plots, we can ask. "Does Belinda still have a chance to dance?" They may say that maybe she has to be a restaurant waitress in her whole life; it's not so bad. Because helping others in a restaurant is also meaningful, there is no need to be frustrated.

Let children continue to read with the method of imagination and verification. Later, Belinda still wanted to dance while working as the restaurant waitress. She often read magazines about dancing and cherished her dream of dancing. When a band came to perform in the restaurant, Belinda began to dance unconsciously with the band's accompaniment. The restaurant owner discovered Belinda's dancing talents and asked her to dance in the restaurant. More and more guests liked her performance, and her dance story soon reached the Grand Metropolitan Ballet. The conductor of the dance group came to the restaurant in admiration. After watching Belinda's dance, the conductor was quite surprised and invited her to join in the Grand Metropolitan Ballet. Belinda achieved a great success at Grand Metropolitan Hall. She danced as much as she liked with charming gestures. Now ask children what would Belinda think? Will she complain about having been jeered at in the past? Will she still feel inferior because of her big feet? Does she think the success came from her perseverance?

The answers can be found on the last page: Belinda was happy because she could dance and dance and dance. As for her past experience, she didn't care a fig.

In this reading process, parents can encourage the children to guess how the story will develop and verify their imagination. There are endless possible plots. In the end, children will understand that Belinda ushered in her ideal life as a result of her passion about dancing and her earnest devotion. Everything she had experienced was a necessary setback to facilitate her growth. Those challenges shaped her into a confident, free, and passionate dancer.

The method of imagination and verification can be used in the reading of most picture books. Imagination is unlimited, but story lines are fixed. Children can verify their guesses by referring to stories and thus adjust their own cognition and values.

Summary

The tool of imagination and verification aims to develop children's abilities to think and reflect, and form the habit of reflecting. It can truly improve children's abilities to read, learn, and think. When reading a picture book, parents can encourage their children to guess based on what they have read. These guesses will be verified or refuted by the progression of the story.

Imagination is unlimited. Children can verify their imagination by referring to stories and thus adjust their own cognition and values.

Chapter 7

Training Children's Expressive Ability Based on Reading

Rehearsal exercise: Why children can't retell after reading so many books

Rehearsal Exercise

When children become familiar with a picture book, parents can encourage them to retell it. Ask children to repeat short sentences literally. For complex sentences, allow children to retell them by processing the original information.

The rehearsal exercise is a basic tool for children to master what they have read. It is usually called reading, reading aloud, or recitation. How best to use this tool in the reading enlightenment of children aged from three to six?

First of all, we must figure out the real goals of rehearsal. It doesn't mean rote learning. We should know that the ultimate purpose of reading is not to fill our brains with endless knowledge. Instead, we should learn to think independently and rationally through reading, and then use these abilities to create a better world. In other words, reading aims not at knowledge input, but at the effective upgrade of cognition, from rehearsal to paraphrase to free output. The "upgrade" should be "effective." A real reader will never parrot or imitate others rigidly. They must be a truly creative expresser and shaper.

A series of studies in the field of brain science show that children already have many basic systems and functions in their brains when they are born. They have innate cognitive talents for numbers, causalities, reasoning, language, and visual memory. These talents are the foundation of rehearsal exercises in reading enlightenment. Without foundational talents, the rehearsal content can't be loaded into the brain; even when loaded, it will be forgotten quickly. Scientific research has discovered that most children have the foundation of more advanced abilities, such as strategy and metacognition. These foundational abilities must be repeatedly stimulated and trained in the period of early reading enlightenment. Thus, children can lay a rock-solid foundation for the middle-to-high-end thinking models needed in school. The rehearsal exercise is important in early reading enlightenment. It's also a key learning strategy for children when they grow up.

The rehearsal exercise is also a necessary mechanism for children to learn language. At an early age, children can distinguish nonverbal stimuli from verbal information in the words of adults, differentiate language changes, and notice the coordination between mouth shapes and sounds. These innate language abilities enable children to speak their mother languages fluently, form concepts, and develop commonsense knowledge about the world at the age of three. Therefore, using rehearsal exercises when reading picture books can help children express and understand many words, phrases, and sentences when they are in elementary school. With a sound training in basic abilities, children can be better prepared for school life. They will use various reading and learning tools learned in school in a more flexible way and meet fewer obstacles in academic development.

Don't make the rehearsal exercise become a burden to children of from three to six years old, or it will be counterproductive. In this period, children can consciously memorize some content, but truly effective learning and memory must be connected with physical movements and experience. The theory of embodied cognition suggests that children's knowledge about the world is determined by their body structures, sense organs, nerves, and exercise patterns. Cognition and intelligence are inseparable from the body; otherwise, they would be meaningless. Therefore, a truly scientific and effective way of learning has much to do with children's personal experience and opportunities to share it with their parents. Therefore, when reading a picture book, parents should ask some questions and repeat their children's answers. They should encourage their children to retell what they have read and to talk about events that happened in their life. These interactions can help children to further expand their commonsense knowledge about the world. The necessary rehearsal and paraphrase training in parent-child reading will deeply influence children's abilities to deal with various challenges. Therefore, parents should learn to use these tools to interact with their children and thus improve children's reading and learning abilities.

꽃

Rehearsal and paraphrase exercises also play an important role in the enlightenment about speaking and reading. However, it's not quite easy to do these seemingly simple exercises, because children are not mature enough.

Rehearsal means to repeat things said by others or oneself. Rehearsal, or retelling a picture book with one's own words, is the most basic tool and method in reading picture books. Ask children to literally repeat simple sentences and guide them to retell complex ones after processing and integrating the original information.

꽃

When doing specific rehearsal exercises, parents should guide their children to:
Change written language into spoken language. Because it's difficult to remember written words in oral retelling, repeating written language means reciting. However, in early reading enlightenment, we can't force children to memorize things by reciting, otherwise they will become averse to reading.

For example, when retelling *Avocado Baby*, say "not tall and not strong" to describe the Hargarves instead of "neither tall nor strong" as in the original text. Such an oral expression is closer to the daily life of children.

Second, highlight key points when retelling. Ask children to summarize a picture book in from one to five sentences and highlight the key points. This can develop their abilities to generalize and catch key points. For example, when retelling *Seven Blind Mice*, children need to know the core of the story. Each mouse only touched one part of a strange something, and finally they knew it was an elephant after exploring the whole strange something. Children should stress that "We shouldn't take a part for the whole. Instead, we should study something from all perspectives."

Third, express things in a clear order. Children need to string together relevant plot points with internal connections and use their own words. When retelling a story, children must clearly tell when, where, why, and how it happened, who is the main character, and what happened in the ending. The method of collating clues can be integrated in this process. For example, when children are retelling *Duck on a Bike*, guide them to talk about the duck's actions when riding the bike, who he met, and what the other animals did. The duck became more and more skilled at riding, and other animals who refused to ride finally accepted it. Children can use this clue to retell the story.

Fourth, retell completely and accurately. The basic requirement of rehearsal is not missing important plots and processes. "Complete" means it shouldn't be fragmented and doesn't interpret plot points out of context. "Accurate" means not giving wrong information and use proper and concise words. However, don't be too worried if a child's rehearsal is wordy at first. Parents can guide them to make it shorter and more accurate.

Fifth, add proper imagination when necessary. Mistakes should be avoided in rehearsal, but it doesn't mean to simply copy and paste. An important aim of rehearsal is to practice expressive ability. So, it can be innovative as long as the original meaning remain unchanged. Innovative rehearsal can effectively practice children's abilities to understand content and to express themselves. For example, when retelling the *Duck on a Bike*, if a child says, "All the animals are riding a bike. The cow can ride without holding the grips. The sheep can stand on the seat with one leg." Here the child reasonably imagines the actions of the cow and sheep, which should be approved and encouraged by the parents.

When children begin to read more complex picture books, teach them several other rehearsal methods:

1. Retell with time-related words.
2. Retell with keywords.
3. Retell with details.
4. Retell creatively with imagination, conception, organization, and creation.
5. Retell based on the beginning, development, climax, and ending of the story.
6. Retell according to story structures. For example, retell narrative plots first and then lyric ones, or from "narrative to descriptive to lyric" parts, or "beginning—transition—turning—ending."
7. Retell from the perspectives of different characters.

In addition, parents can also teach children to retell different types of picture books with different strategies.

1. For plot-based books, retell based on the beginning, development, climax, and ending of the story.

2. For true stories, retell based on when, where, who, why, how, and what the results were.
3. For lyric picture books, guide children to retell from narrative to lyric parts, or from descriptive to lyric parts, and stress the characteristics of "cohesive theme under dispersing description."

Of course, any rehearsal can be adjusted according to local conditions and timing. In early reading enlightenment, as long as the essence of the original text is not changed, children can choose any above method to retell. Innovative rehearsal can be tried later when children's relevant abilities have improved.

Summary

Reading aims not at knowledge input, but at the effective upgrade of cognitive abilities, from rehearsal to paraphrase to free output. It's a key in early reading enlightenment and a necessary mechanism for children to learn language.

In rehearsal exercises, parents should guide children to change written language into spoken language, highlight key points and retell them in a clear order, retell completely and accurately, and add proper imagination when necessary.

Jump-back rehearsal: What to do if children often forget when retelling stories

Jump-Back Rehearsal

When encountering a plot that has something to do with previous plots or details, parents can jump back to review them with their children. This is the method of jump-back rehearsal. Rehearsal can strengthen memory. Jumping back can improve the ability to rehearse content.

Any information we receive through listening or reading will leave an impression on us, but the impression may later become incomplete. To increase its efficiency, the brain will selectively keep some information based on degree of importance. Unimportant information, such as things we see unintentionally, will be quickly deleted. So, if we don't repeat important information in a certain way, our memory of it will be very dim.

In early reading enlightenment of children, it's necessary to repeat important information. Jump-back rehearsal is designed for this. Rehearsal can strengthen memory, and jumping back can improve the ability to rehearse content. It's actually very easy to use this method. When encountering a plot that has something to do with previous plots or details, parents can jump back to review them with their children. By repeatedly jumping back and doing more rehearsals, children can from a positive cycle of information input and output in the same way that repeating breathing can strengthen the functioning of the heart and lungs.

We adults seem to suffer from amnesia in many daily occasions. For instance, we suddenly forget the name of a familiar picture book, a well-remembered ancient poem, the location of a key we just put down. . . . We actually didn't forget, because the memory will come back after a while. Just at that very moment, it failed us. This is not amnesia, but a failure to retrieve memory, which is very common.

Research in brain science shows that forgetting is a self-protection mechanism of the brain, because if too much information is stored in the brain, it will seriously affect our mental health. Therefore, when we forget something momentarily, relevant information codes are not erased completely. If don't want that crash, we need to repeatedly retell relevant information to smoothen the retrieval process. Therefore, we should often use the method of jump-back rehearsal when reading picture books. It can reinforce children's memory and improve reading effects. At the same time, their reading habits and abilities will also improve.

Rehearsal means to tell what one has read or heard in his/her own words. This is a simple but effective reading method. Charlotte Mason, a famous British educator, recommended it to parents and children and believed it can truly help children to understand a picture book and develop good reading habits. Her theory divided children's brains into an external area and an internal area. The former stores short-term memory that has nothing to do with moral character. The latter stores long-term memory, which is the foundation of children's qualities and cognition. When information and knowledge enter the internal area, they are no longer simply stored there. They will be understood and used by children and as a result, they determine how smart a child is.

Rehearsal is a very effective learning method, but parents should know two secrets of the brain in order to truly understand how to use it.

First, the brain needs to break the familiarity illusion. The brain will have a memory illusion that easily takes "familiarity" as "proficiency" by mistake, so it may regard familiar information as information that has been remembered. For example, children feel happy when listening to a story. They think they are familiar with it after listening to it several times. However, if asked to retell it without the book, they generally can't manage to do so easily. Therefore, without other reading tools, children will stay in the comfort zone of information input. It will be easier for the brain to obtain information and harder for it to extract information. In other words, the easier it is for children to remember information, the more difficult it is to retell that information. Therefore, parents should frequently use the method of jump-back rehearsal when reading a picture book. It can stimulate children's brains to work actively and increase the difficulty of information input. Thus, it will be less difficult to retrieve information, and the child's memories will be better consolidated.

Second, avoid "rote rehearsal." Many parents say their children can only reply to closed questions by "yes" or "no," but can't deal with open-ended questions, let alone rehearsal, which is more difficult. Some parents say their children can retell simple information by imitation, but easily forgot it. Such retelling is called maintenance rehearsal, simple rehearsal, or rote rehearsal. In this process, the briefly memorized information is only repeatedly and simply processed by the brain. The memory for it can be reinforced, but it is unlikely to become a long-term memory, because no knowledge chain has been formed. In other words, children only remember some simple information by rote, but there is no relation between different pieces of information. It's also not connected with children's original information. Therefore, it can only be briefly memorized and thus easily forgotten.

Therefore, rehearsal can have real effects only if information and knowledge are connected with each other through effectively jumping back. This kind of rehearsal is also called elaborative rehearsal. It can further process and organize briefly memorized information and establish a stable relationship between it and the information originally stored in the brain. Thus, the information can be transferred into the area of long-term memory.

★

How to Properly Use the Method of Jump-Back Rehearsal

First, help children choose a proper picture book. High-quality picture books can provide excellent classic stories. The authors must have devoted much effort to these books, and they can inspire children's desire for reading and learning interesting stories.

Second, let children learn simple rehearsal, elaborative rehearsal, and creative rehearsal successively. Children from three to six years old can retell short stories At first, let children choose books with simple story lines and relatively short content, such as *Good Night, Gorilla*, and retell them. When children become skilled at simple rehearsal, guide them to jump back in the same book and then among many books.

Read to children with patience, and encourage them to repeat what they have heard in their own words. Stop at the proper time, so as to give them some time to digest what they have heard and then retell it. Don't give any comment before they finish retelling. After children finish it, help them sort out information, find the relationship between plot points and other details, and then encourage them to perform innovative rehearsal by themselves.

Third, teach children certain rehearsal skills. We have introduced some skills in detail in last section, so here is only a brief review. Parents should help children to convert written words into spoken words. When children are retelling a story, guide them to accurately highlight key points, express them in a clear order, and grasp the internal connections between relevant parts. To retell a complete plot, they must show when, where, why, and how it happened, who is the main character, and the result. At the same time, they should gradually learn to retell with accurate words.

Fourth, teach children to integrate memorizing, thinking, and expressing activities in the process of rehearsal. Memory is the foundation of rehearsal. So, in order to retell well, children should learn to read and memorize something at the same time and use their mouths and brains together. Rehearsal can strengthen memory, but don't do it by rote. Parents should guide their children to reorganize, keep, or delete the content of a picture book and organize their words to retell it. Frequent rehearsal can not only strengthen children's memory but also improve their ability to think. Children should retell stories fluently and introduce the core aspects and outlines accurately and clearly. Output and expression are the ultimate goals of reading and retelling.

Summary

Parents can often use the method of jump-back rehearsal in the parent-child reading of picture books. It can reinforce children's memory. At the same time, children's reading habits and abilities will also become better. When retelling stories, children should break the familiarity illusion, stimulate their brains to work actively, and increase the difficulty of information input. They should also avoid "rote rehearsal," establish certain relationships between information, and carry out elaborative rehearsal.

To use the method of jump-back rehearsal properly, parents should guide their children to: First, choose a proper picture book. Second, learn simple rehearsal, then elaborative rehearsal, and finally creative rehearsal. Third, master certain rehearsal skills. Fourth, integrate memorizing, thinking, and expressing activities when retelling stories.

Adaptation and continuation: Should we encourage children to invent stories when reading?

Adaptation and Continuation

When children can understand a story, their parents can guide them to adapt or continue it. To make a good adaptation and continuation, children should clearly know the causes, processes, and ending of a story. As compared with reading, adaptation and continuation are a new kind of output.

They are middle-to-high-level methods for early reading enlightenment, because many abilities, including comprehension, logical thinking, language organization and expression, imagination and communication, are involved. It is generally recommended to start adaptation and continuation (A&C) when children are older than five. A&C has extraordinary significance in improving children's reading and expressive abilities at the early stage.

First, A&C can stimulate children's interest in reading and enlighten them about writing. Understanding is the key of improving children's interest in reading. That is, it is possible for them to adapt and continue a story after they can understand it. When children are guided to adapt and continue a story, they can understand its story lines and character relationships more deeply. When reprocessing a story, they are forcing themselves to gain a deeper understanding. They can also know its causes, processes, and the ending more clearly by collating plots and memorizing the story outline. As compared with reading, A&C is a new kind of output, or creation.

In the process of parent-child reading, parents turn pictures and words into invisible language. Children learn to understand the visible pictures and words by listening to invisible language. Then, they change the visible information into invisible language through A&C. In this process, they can establish a bridge between reading and writing, without relying on words. Writing is actually a reverse engineering of reading, so A&C is also the initial stage of children's ability to write.

Second, A&C helps children develop their logical thinking. When just beginning to read, children may find it difficult to understand the coherence of plots. They can't establish key linear logical relationships. The information they received is like scattered pearls without a string. Establishing a logical relationship means to string dispersed pieces information on the thread of logic. Children need to be trained in this ability. Children with poor logical thinking tend to show messy logic in oral communication and the reports or articles written by them. A complete story must have basic elements, such as the beginning, development processes, and the ending. There is also a logical relationship between previous and following plots. When adapting, children need to reorganize the story's logical relationship, which will effectively practice their ability to think logically.

Third, A&C helps to develop children's abilities to organize language and express themselves. Encourage children to read picture books with their parents, then read by themselves, and finally make up stories or write something based on pictures. When reading picture books to children who are too young to know written words, parents are telling stories with their own language, and the children are listening. In this process, they are reading pictures, and their brains are learning how to change these pictures into words. The pictures in excellent picture books are good at telling stories. While reading pictures, children are also listening to the stories. Their ears and eyes are working together, which can allow them practice their preliminary abilities of reading written words and speaking. They can't do this by themselves.

When parents are reading to them, the language world children hear and see will overlap, though there may be some subtle differences. Thus, children can finish the basic training and enlightenment about reading through listening to their parents reading. Therefore, when children have reached certain levels of reading, we can guide them to make up stories. It can make a good use of the language and reading foundation laid before in parent-child reading and further improve their abilities to organize language and express themselves. If parents want their children to tell stories with proper tones and relatively complex sentences, they should provide guidance. At the beginning of A&C training, children may use improper words and logic. It doesn't matter; just let them express what they want to and don't interrupt. Parents should correct them in a proper manner after they have finished their work.

Fourth, A&C helps stimulate children's imagination. If listening to stories is receiving regular training in logical inference and a process of stringing the pearls, adapting stories is then equal to scattering the pearls and threading them again with a different pattern. This process, from divergent thinking to concentrated thinking and to divergent thinking again, can further inspire children's imagination. Don't put any restrictions on children's adaptation of stories. Let them break the routine, use their wild imagination, and show their surprising creativity. Because children at this age have an instinct to mismatch, which is a process of building linguistic and logical systems through trial and error and a process of fully experiencing the charm of creation. So, random mismatches have a long-term impact on the development of children's basic language skills and imagination.

Fifth, A&C can promote the parent-child relationship. From telling stories and reading picture books, to making up stories, parents and children are actively interacting and cooperating with each other to create life experiences. In most cases, these experiences will be engraved in children's minds and enhance family affections. Machi Tawara, a well-known Japanese poet, published a best-selling collection of poems at the age of twenty-six. Her language skills are extraordinary. In childhood, Machi Tawara asked her mom to read picture books for her every day. The same collection of folk stories was often read repeatedly, and some stories were told hundreds of times. At the age of three, she once retold all of the stories in a book by referring to the pictures, although she was illiterate at that time. Her mother was greatly surprised. This unique experience remains fresh in her memory even after decades. The process of parent-child reading not only allowed her to have amazing writing skills, but also created an unforgettable family experience.

❈

A&C is of great significance for children's growth. Then, what should parents do at home to make a good use of this tool?

An example that comes to mind is the classic story named *The True Story of the Three Little Pigs*, which was adapted from the folk story *The Three Little Pigs*. In the original story, the three little pigs have grown up, so their mom asks them to build their own houses. The first pig built a straw house, the second built a wooden house, and the third built a brick house. A big wicked wolf wanted to eat the three pigs, so he came to the straw house and blew it down. Then, the first pig was eaten. The wolf then came to the wooden house and blew it down again. So, the second pig was also eaten. The wolf finally came to the brick house, but it stood firmly no matter how hard he blew. So, he decided to get in through the chimney. However, the third pig was heating water under the chimney, and the wolf fell into the pot full of boiling water. As a result, the wolf was eaten by the third pig.

The cover of *The True Story of the Three Little Pigs* is a picture of *Daily Wolf*, a newspaper. The front-page headline is "The True Story of Three Little Pigs," which was told by the wolf. The whole book is made up with the reports about interviewing the big wolf. In an interview, the wolf appealed for redressing the "injustice." He said the first story about the three little pigs was not true. According to the wolf, he went to his neighbor 's house to borrow some sugar. He had a bad cold that day, so he sneezed when he arrived at the door of the first pig's house. Then, the straw house just fell down and crushed the pig to death. So, he ate it. Then, he went to the house of the second pig for sugar. Again, just after a sneeze, the house fell down, and the pig died. So, he ate the second pig. Finally, he went to the house of the third pig and sneezed, and luckily the house didn't fall down. However, the pig was very impolite and slandered him. So, he became angry about it. At that moment, the police and reporters came, and the wolf was arrested. But the reporters thought the story of borrowing sugar was not exciting, so they distorted the facts and made up that fake story.

Parents can read both stories to their children, in order to inspire them to adapt stories.

Second, the materials that can be adapted include not only picture books, but also nursery rhymes, children's songs, and any other interesting things in life. Parents should encourage their children to adapt and continue any materials they are familiar with. If parents have heard their children making up and adapting poetry and popular nursery rhymes, they will know that children are actually gifted with interesting adaptation. But as parents, we need to master certain methods and establish certain rules to guide our children to make meaningful A&C in a scientific way.

The following methods can be used to guide children's creation.

First, encourage children to describe pictures. This is also an important method for enlightening student of lower grade in primary schools about their writing. We can let children make up a short story based on any picture. For example, on seeing a picture of a water glass, we can guide them to make up a story about the world in the glass. It can give a full play to their imagination.

Second, play interactive adaptation games with children. Combine the process of adaptation with interactive games, such as sentence solitaire. Parents make up a sentence, and children continue it with another sentence. Words solitaire or other games can also be played during this process. Children can highly involve themselves in these games, so they will be more interested in the adaptation. As a result, they will make up better stories and receive better training effects.

Third, guide children with heuristic methods. This is designed mainly for children who can't retell or adapt a whole story. For these children, we should inspire them to retell or adapt sentences one by one with their imagination. Parents should play a leading role in this process to guide their children. Ask questions and guide them at proper time to inspire their imagination. Encourage them on sight of any spark of wit, so that they can have more confidence in and desires for expression.

Fourth, encourage children to make contrastive adaptation. After reading through a picture book, find other picture books or cartoons that have certain relations to it. Ask children to exchange the main characters and combine the plots of the two stories. For example, after reading over *The True Story of the Three Little Pigs* with children, we can let them imagine what will happen if the Peppa Pig meets that wolf? We can even encourage them to put themselves or their friends into a story. It can motivate them to take part in the adaptation and develop their narrative abilities to control multiple characters and structures.

Fifth, don't force children to adapt or continue stories. The method of A&C aims to generate their interest in reading. They will turn averse to it if being forced to do so. As a result, parents will find it quite hard to complete the reading enlightenment for their children. Try to combine A&C with funny games, and don't make reckless remarks or criticisms. Parents should be active mentors, loyal listeners, and good recorders. When children are telling a story adapted by them, we should take a video of it. When they grow older, they can review that video and find more confidence from it. The record will also become a precious memory about their childhood.

Summary

Adaptation and continuation are good for training children's reading and expressing abilities. They also play a significant role in the improvement of children's logical thinking, imagination, and comprehension. Children can adapt and continue picture books, nursery rhymes, children's songs, and any other interesting things they experience in life. However, don't make up illogical stories. Parents should guide their children to create stories effectively by means of picture description, interactive adaptation games, heuristic guidance, and contrastive adaptation.

Comprehensive output: Why children can't write good essays even after reading many books

Comprehensive Output

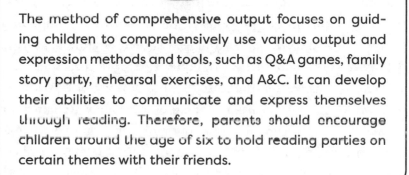

The method of comprehensive output focuses on guiding children to comprehensively use various output and expression methods and tools, such as Q&A games, family story party, rehearsal exercises, and A&C. It can develop their abilities to communicate and express themselves through reading. Therefore, parents should encourage children around the age of six to hold reading parties on certain themes with their friends.

There are four core skills for children to learn language: listening, speaking, reading, and writing. The four skills are matched to four basic progressive processes: listening to, telling, reading, and writing stories. Listening and reading are input training; speaking and writing are output training. We tend to value input and think input decides output. In fact, they are of equal importance. One of the purposes of reading is to shape one's output abilities of speaking and writing.

For children from three to six, there is no need to give too much emphasis to writing training. After children have attended school, writing exercises will be gradually advanced from picture description to normal writing with certain topics. For children from three to six years old, writing training should focus on a series of communication and expression exercises based on the reading of picture books.

We have shared more than twenty reading tools suitable for children aged from three to six in the previous chapters and sections. Many of them are designed for output and expression training, such as Q&A games, family story party, rehearsal exercises, and A&C. These tools can improve children's abilities to communicate and express themselves. The method of comprehensive output emphasizes how to use previous methods and tools comprehensively. To this end, we can encourage children of around six years old to hold reading parties on certain themes with their friends.

Why emphasize comprehensive output? Many of the output-based reading tools mentioned before are mainly designed for output and expression exercises, most of which are carried out between a parent and a child, or among several family members. Many parents may strongly feel that their children are good talkers at home but are too shy to show themselves in public. It is a very common phenomenon. In addition to children's personalities, are there any other causes? The main reason is: the public environment is real, and the real world is three-dimensional and very complex. However, communication and expression in family environment are generally single-dimensional and inapplicable to the complex and three-dimensional real world. It also essentially explains why most of us can't apply our knowledge in real life.

Most international brain scientists and cognitive psychologists believe that this problem is caused by improper input training. Only diversified and alternate training can improve cognition and expression abilities. To make it easy to understand, if what we input is always superficial and monotonous, our memory, understanding, and cognition will be very unreliable; only complex and difficult input can truly enhance the abilities to read, learn, and express. From this point of view, it is easy to understand that comprehensive output can effectively shape children's abilities to live in a complex world.

＊

Then, how to truly improve children's various abilities? Give them complex output exercises directly from the beginning? Obviously, it doesn't work. Too-complex expression training will only make children more reluctant to speak, because if it's too difficult for them to finish a "task," they will become indifferent to that task, or even psychologically resist all other "tasks" related to it.

Given this, the expression exercises we introduced before should also be gradually advanced from easy to difficult. Q&A games are a very basic expression exercise, where children can feel the pleasure of thinking and are rewarded for actively asking and answering questions. Thus, they can gradually take part in in-depth communication during the process of reading. With the improvement of expressive abilities, children become capable of simple rehearsals, and then A&C, role-play, and family story party.

These progressive reading methods are designed according to children's expressive abilities, so when using them, parents should consider their children's specific situations and make corresponding changes. However, they must move to the stage of comprehensive output eventually. To be specific, for children older than six, parents should often use the method of comprehensive output on picture books or literature works for children that are worth intensive reading. Thus, children can really adapt themselves to difficult graded reading based on the previous stage of training.

The relationship between listening and reading and speaking and writing is essentially about efficiency of information input and output. Comprehensive output means to comprehensively use various reading methods to correct children's consensus errors that may occur when they are outputting information. What does "consensus error" mean? It means whether children's understanding of information is consistent with that of others when they express it to others. If not, there is a consensus error. If we can reduce the error rate by various means, the accuracy rate of children's reading comprehension and expression will be improved. It's obvious that influential figures not only have few errors in understanding and expression, but also can surpass superficial understanding and cognition and penetrate into people's hearts. Therefore, they can create great literary works and works in other realms of expression, such as television and film. Teaching the method of comprehensive output is actually a process of information exchange that may be private, small-scale, or large-scale. Such interaction can reduce children's error rate of expression.

When children are about five or six years old, their parents can also encourage them to hold public reading activities on certain themes with their friends. Before starting these activities, parents and children need to make reading preparation in three aspects.

First, encourage children to read after parents and then read by themselves. At first, children read after their parents and answer relevant questions to interact with their parents. It can help them to fully understand the book. Then, encourage them to read through a book without guidance and retell it as much as they can. In this process, children first listen to their parents reading, then they tell the story to themselves, and finally they can read through it independently. It is a necessary scientific transition from reading after others to reading by themselves. This kind of training should be often carried out to enlighten children from three to six years old about their reading. So, parents must be patient.

Second, encourage children in independent reading and then autonomous expression. When children can read simple content by themselves, we can train them for basic expressive abilities with effective methods. They can thus effectively memorize what they have read by digesting and collating it on their own. It is a necessary process for children to test their knowledge and think independently. As mentioned before, the information received by parents may be different from what children have expressed. Parents, as listeners, need to interpret the information they have heard, so there may be some misunderstandings caused by incomplete, illogical, or inaccurate expression. Therefore, parents must listen carefully to the expression of their children, without interrupting recklessly. If children stumble, we can give some hints, but don't let them parrot what we say. They can gradually form their own habits of expression and improve their expressing abilities through frequent training.

Third, encourage children in autonomous expression in an unfamiliar environment. In a familiar environment, they will be encouraged even if having made a mistake. But in an unfamiliar circumstance, they worry at being laughed at or looked down if they have made any mistakes. They feel less secure, so their expressive abilities decrease.

In elementary school, the teachers encourage their students to tell stories or perform on a stage. Most children only have several chances for public expression in a year, which is finished by reciting. They have good short-term memory and can fluently recite or express certain content, so they will win applause and encouragement. Therefore, although reciting is far from fluent autonomous expression, it can make children feel more confident of expressing something in a strange environment.

In addition to the above, encourage children to play storytelling games with their friends. In this circumstance, they will feel more nervous than having a family story party, but much easier than expressing something in a class. In this process of storytelling, the host parents should encourage children to think and discuss deeply, and speak freely. Children's valuable ideas should be highly praised. If getting positive feedback about their thinking and expression results, they will become more enthusiastic about thinking and expression. Then, their reading and expression skills can be truly improved. If such an activity can be organized once a month, the scope of children's public expression can be expanded to a certain extent. When children are from five to six years old, they will gradually become able to express themselves in public based on the experience accumulated in previous reading parties.

It's not easy for adults, let alone children, to express themselves perfectly in public. However, it is a necessary core ability. It can't be cultivated in one or two days, so we have to train for it from an early age. The method of comprehensive output can help children to talk about the books they have read and carefully listen to the speech of others. It can improve the effects and meaning of reading. From the above three kinds of preparation, we can find: the most important point is not children's reactions in reading activities, but the *interaction* between parents and children. The mechanism of response is a key to children's comprehensive output. Giving responses is actually a process of effective discussion. A discussant should tell their thoughts to others, digest what others have said, and sort out their real opinions by referring to other viewpoints.

Everyone can improve their thinking ability through full expression. This is also the most effective way to develop children's abilities of comprehension, analysis, expression, and generalization.

Summary

The real world is three-dimensional and very complex. However, communication and expression in the family environment are generally single-dimensional and unsuited for coping with the complex and three-dimensional real world. The method of comprehensive output can effectively shape children's abilities to live in a complex world. When children are about five or six years old, the parents can also encourage them to hold public reading activities on certain themes with their friends. Before starting these activities, make reading preparation in three aspects: encourage children to read after parents and then read by themselves; encourage children in independent reading and then autonomous expression; and encourage children in autonomous expression in an unfamiliar environment.

The mechanism of response is a key to children's comprehensive output. Parents should encourage children to think and discuss deeply and speak freely. Their valuable ideas should be highly praised. If getting positive feedback about their thinking and expression results, they will become more enthusiastic about thinking and expression.

Further Reading

Angry Arthur by Hiawyn Oram

Avocado Baby by John Burningham

The Biggest Cake in the World by Joy Cowley

Belinda The Ballerina by Amy Young

Create Super Children Brains by Big J

A Dark, Dark Tale by Ruth Brown

Decisive: How to Make Better Choices in Life and Work by Chip and Dan Heath

Don't Let the Pigeon Drive the Bus by Mo Willems

Duck on a Bike by David Shannon

The Elephant and the Bad Baby by Elfrida Vipont

Four Thirty by Yin Shizhong

Giggle King's Big Hat by Edward Lear

Good Night, Gorilla by Peggy Rathmann

The Gruffalo by Julia Donaldson

Harry the Dirty Dog by Gene Zoin

Jim Trelease's The Read-Aloud Handbook by Jim Trelease

Last Stop on Market Street by Matt de la Peña

The Lightning Fish Named Nick by Fang Suzhen

The Little Prince by Antoine de Saint-Expuery

Make Way for Ducklings by Robert McCloskey

Martine at the Farm by Marcei Marlier and Gilbert Delahaye

Miss Rumphius by Barbara Cooney

Mole and the Baby Bird by Marjorie Newman

Molly Goes Shopping by Eva Eriksson

My Dad! by Anthony Browne

Olivia by Ian Falconer

Peter's Chair by Ezra Jack Keats

The Pigeon Needs a Bath by Mo Willems

The Polar Express by Chris Van Allsburg

Poo-Poo by Shuntaro Tanikawa

The Rainbow Flower by Xing Fuzhongzi

The Rhinoceros Horn of Sudan by Dai Yun

Sapiens: A Brief History of Humankind by Yuval Noah Harari

Seven Blind Mice by Ed Young

A Taste of the Moon by Michael Grejniec

The Three Robbers by Tomi Ungerer

Titch by Pat Hutchins

The True Story of the Three Little Pigs by Jon Scieszka

Index

Page numbers followed by f refer to figures and those followed by t refer to tables.

A

abstract objects, 7–10, 8f, 9f, 10f, 13
adaptation and continuation, 185–192
addiction, science of, 81–82
age
  behavioral features by, 139t–142t
  cognitive development characteristics
    by, 147t
alternate reading, 101–107
Angry Arthur, 27–30, 153
animal research, 81, 117
Arbib, Michael A., 119
attention management, 39–46
augmented-reality technology, 47–48
autonomous expression, 197
Avocado Baby, 175

B

Baby Bear book series, 74
Bauer, Patricia, 61, 63
behavior adjustment, 136–143
behavioral features, by age, 139t–142t
Belinda the Ballerina, 168–170
Berridge, Kent, 81
The Biggest Cake in the World, 153, 159–164

book suitability, by age, 139t–142t
brain remodeling, 136
brain science
  of addiction, 81–82
  of attention, 39–42
  of behavior adjustment, 136–137
  childhood memory research, 61–63
  of familiarity illusion, 181
  of forgetting, 180
  of foundational abilities, 173
  of graded reading training, 96
  of language development, 76–77
  of listening to stories, 1–2
  memory-related, 33–35
  of mind mapping, 158–159
  mirror neurons and role play, 117–119
  of narrative needs and speculative ability,
    55–56
  of participation, 99
  of recitation, 109, 112
  of self-examination and self-adjustment,
    166–167
  of self mode *vs.* stranger model, 133
  of sensory input and learning, 49
  text brain section, 96–97

Index

Brown, Peter C., 101–102
Browne, Anthony, 201
bubble maps, 160
Bush, Barbara, 111
Buzan, Tony, 158

C
circle maps, 159–160
clues, collation of, 151–156
cognition, embodied, 174
cognitive development, 146–150, 147t
cognitive theory on alternate practice,
    101–103
collation of clues, 151–156
commitments to reading, 71–72
comparisons, making, 12–13, 16, 20–21
comprehension
    adaptation and continuation after,
        185–186
    collation of clues, 151–156
    gestures for not understanding, 57–58
    imagination and verification, 166–171
    milestone method, 144–150
    picture reading and, 10–11
    plot maps, 157–165
concentrated thinking, 124
connecting questions, 4–5
consensus errors, 196
content repetition approach, 32–38, 62–63
context and the word-locking approach,
    90, 91
contrastive adaptation, 191
Create Super Children Brains, 126

D
daily scenes and Q&A games, 127
A Dark, Dark Tale, 35–37
Decisive, 149
deliberate vs. alternate practice, 102–103
designated reading time and place, 70–71
details. See page-to-detail approach
distributed-reading practice, 103–104
divergent thinking, 124, 129
diversified-reading practice, 105–106

double bubble maps, 161–162
Duck on a Bike, 98, 155, 176–177
dyslexia, 87–88

E
Eight Steps of Learning to Read, 11t
electronic devices, 41
The Elephant and the Bad Baby, 138
embodied cognition, 174
emotion comparison cards, 23–31, 25f
emotions, 13, 42, 62
empathy training, 26
expert guidance and parent-child reading,
    131–135
expressive ability
    adaptation and continuation, 185–192
    comprehensive output, 193–199
    family story parties, 93–100
    jump-back rehearsal, 179–184
    rehearsal exercise, 172–178
eye contact, 50

F
familiarity illusion, 181
family story parties, 93–100, 195
Fang Suzhen, 139
Fei Xiaotong, 67
finger-reading, 75
flash cards, 13
flow maps, 163–164
foundational abilities, 173
Four Thirty, 154–155
frequency, question, 5

G
games and adaptation, 190
gestures for not understanding, 57–58
Giggle King's Big Hat, 4–6
goal management, 81, 84, 85
Good Night, Gorilla, 182
graded reading
    emotion comparison cards in, 30
    imagination and verification in,
        167–171

language development and, 76
phased targeting in, 80
purpose of, 94
"Graded Reading on Good Character and
Scholarship," 17, 96
Greenfield, Patricia Marks, 119
The Gruffalo, 13

H

habituation, 81–82
Harari, Yuval Noah, 97
Harry the Dirty Dog, 63–65
Harvard University, 95
Heath, Chip, 149
Heath, Dan, 149
hemispheres, brain, 33–34, 96, 157
heuristic methods of adaptation, 190–191
holistic questioning, 2, 3
Hometown China, 67

I

imagination
in adaptation and continuation,
187–188
attention management and, 39–46
in rehearsal, 176–177
speculation and, 57
verification and, 166–171
imitation. *See* role play
immersive reading approach, 47–53
independent reading, 197
inference, 128, 166
information-output capacity, 94
instant rewards and phased targeting, 80,
84–85
interaction, parent-child, 15–16, 52, 198
interactive games, 190
interest in reading, developing an, 67,
110–111, 185–186, 191
intermittent questioning, 2–6

J

judgment-based Q&A games, 128–129
jump-back rehearsal, 179–184

K

keyword finding, 12

L

language development
adaptation and continuation in,
186–187
rehearsal exercise and, 174
stepped lead-in reading and, 74–79
Last Stop on Market Street, 104, 153
lead-in reading, stepped, 74–79
Lear, Edward, 200
learned helplessness, 2
learning and practice method types,
103–106
The Lightning Fish Named Nick, 154
listening to stories and brain activity, 1–2
The Little Prince, 72
logical thinking, 62, 186

M

Make Way for Ducklings, 88–91
Martine on the Farm, 13
Mason, Charlotte, 180
material rewards, 83
medal rewards for reaching milestone, 148
memory and recall
childhood memory loss, 61–63
content-repetition and, 33–37
forgetting, 180
speculative ability and, 55–56
mid-way questioning, 2, 3
milestone method, 144–150
mind mapping, 158–159
mirror neurons, 117–119
Mischel, Walter, 132–133
Miss Rumphius, 18–21, 104
Mole and the Baby Bird, 104
Molly Goes Shopping, 3
multidimensional competition, 51
My Dad!, 13

N

narration-based Q&A games, 126–127

narrative needs of the brain, 55
National Association for the Education of
    Young Children, 146
negative reinforcement, 159
neurochemistry and addiction, 81
nursery rhymes, 35, 62–63, 109

O
objects, comparing pictures and, 7–14
observations by children, 16
Olivia, 57
open-ended questions, 4

P
page-to-detail approach, 15–22
paraphrase training, 174–175
parent-child reading
    adaptation and continuation in,
        186–187
    benefits of, 108–112
    brain activity and, 1–2
    expert guidance method of, 131–135
    eye contact during, 50
    imagination and verification in,
        166–171
    intermittent questioning and, 2–6
    methods for, 103–106
    page-to-detail approach, 15–22
    phased-targeting approach in, 84–85
    plot-connection approach, 60–65
    Q&A games with, 123–130
    rehearsal and paraphrase training in,
        174–175
    ritual in, 69–73
    stepped lead-in reading, 77–79
    stepped lead-in reading approach, 74–79
    tips for, 13–15
parent-child relationship, 188
parental behavioral guidance, by child's age,
    139t–142t
participation in family story parties, 99
passive information reception, 1–2
"Peak-End Rule," 149
Peter's Chair, 11–13

phased targeting, 80–85
physiological changes in the brain, 96
picture books
    clue collation and, 153–156
    content-repetition approach using, 33,
        35–37
    emotion comparison card use for, 23–31
    family story parties using, 98–99
    immersive reading approach using,
        47–53
    methods for reading practice, 103–106
    page-to-detail approach using, 15–22
    parent-child reading, 1–6
    picture-to-object approach using, 7–14
picture reading, 10–14
picture-to-object approach, 7–14
The Pigeon Needs a Bath, 125–130
plot and clue collation, 151–156
plot-connection approach, 60–66
plot maps, 157–165
poems, 35, 108, 109
The Polar Express, 133–135
Poo-Poo, 74
positive reinforcement, 69, 159. See also
    rewards
progress and the milestone method,
    144–150
progressive inquiry process, 19
psychology of ritual, 68–70
public expression, 197–198

Q
Q&A games, 123–130, 195
questions
    to encourage speculation, 56–57
    intermittent, 2–6
    picture-to-object approach, 12–13

R
The Rainbow Flower, 153–154
The Read-Aloud Handbook, 110, 113–114
reading after parents, 196–197
reading aloud. See parent-child reading
reading enlightenment

for behavior adjustment, 137–138
imagination and verification and, 168
milestone method in, 144–150
reciting as method of, 109, 110–111
role play and, 121
reading rituals, 67–73
reasoning-based Q&A games, 127–128
reciting, 197–198
reciting fluently, 113–115
reduplication, 74–75, 77–78
rehearsal, 172–178, 179–184, 195
relational comparisons, 20–21
repetition, 32–38, 62–63, 179–180
retelling stories, 172, 174–176, 179–184,
   196–197
reward system of the brain, 40, 42
rewards. *See also* positive reinforcement
   in phased targeting, 80, 82–85
   for reaching milestone, 148
The Rhinoceros Horn of Sudan, 104
ritual-of-reading approach, 67–73
Rizzolatti, Giacomo, 117–118
role play, 98, 116–122, 195
rote rehearsal, avoidance of, 181–182
rules for reading time, 71–72

S
Sapiens: A Brief History of Humankind, 97
self-adjustment, 166–168
self-control, 41, 82–83, 84–85, 137–138
self-examination, 166–167
self mode, 133
self-monitoring, 57–58
self-reward and phased targeting, 82–85
semantic discrimination and brain
   development, 77
senses, 44, 45, 49–53
Seven Blind Mice, 176
shaping behaviors. *See* behavior adjustment
Shizhong, Yin, 200
Skinner, B. F., 69, 159
Snow, Catherine E., 95
speculation approach, 54–59
Sperry, Roger Wolcott, 33
stepped lead-in reading, 74–79

steps to learning to read, 11t
storytelling
   family story parties, 93–100
   games with friends, 198
stranger model, 133
Supercharge a Kid's Brainpower, 11, 23, 49

T
Tanikawa, Shuntaro, 201
A Taste of the Moon, 43–45
Tawara, Machi, 188
technology, immersion-inducing, 47–48
themes, book, 5, 17, 20–21
Thomas, Mark, 110–111
The Three Robbers, 153
Titch, 104
tree maps, 163
Trelease, Jim, 110, 113
The True Story of the Three Little Pigs,
   188–190, 191

U
University of Illinois, 108

V
Van Gennep, Arnold, 67
verification and imagination, 166–171
video recording, 149, 191
virtual reality technology, 48
vocabulary, 13, 88–92

W
whole-brain education, 157
Willems, Mo, 125
word blindness, 87
word-by-word reading, avoiding, 78
word-locking approach, 86–92
writing training, 193–199

X
Xiong Liang, 15

Y
Yamamoto, Yohji, 131